Contingency Planning

IT Infrastructure Library

LONDON: THE STATIONERY OFFICE

Central Computer and Telecommunications Agency

ISBN 0 11 330524 9
ISSN 0956 2591

All references in this book to
'PROMPT' should be taken to read
'PRINCE'. 'PRINCE' is the name of the
CCTA's own recommended Project
Management Method. It is based on
'PROMPT', a proprietary methodology
owned by LBMS PLC. Unlike
'PROMPT', no licence is required to
use the 'PRINCE' methodology.

This is one of the books in the IT
Infrastructure Library series.

For further information on CCTA
products, contact:

CCTA Library
Rosebery Court
St Andrews Business Park
Norwich, NR7 0HS
Telephone 01603 704 930
GTN: 3040 4930

This document has been produced
using procedures conforming to
BSI 5750 Part 1: 1987
ISO 9001:1987

Preface   **vii**

Synopsis   **ix**

1.   Management Summary   **1**

1.1   If It's Not Worth Protecting It's Not Worth Doing!   1
1.2   "It Won't Happen To Me"   1
1.3   Why do Contingency Planning?   1
1.4   How Does This Module Help?   1
1.5   Structure of Module   2

2.   Introduction   **3**

2.1   Target readership   3
2.2   Scope   3
2.3   Context   3
2.4   Related Guidance   4
2.5   Definitions   5
2.6   The Need for Contingency Planning   6
2.7   Statistics on Disasters   7
2.8   Management and Departmental Commitment   8

3.   Planning: The Preliminary Stage   **9**

3.1   Procedures   10
3.1.1 IT Strategy   10
3.1.2 Preliminary Stage: Terms of Reference   10
3.1.3 Preliminary Stage   10
3.1.4 Contingency Options   12
3.1.5 Dormant Contracts   17
3.1.6 Management Approval to Proceed   18
3.1.7 Set up the Project Team   18
3.1.8 Project Management   18
3.2   Dependencies   18
3.3   People   18
3.3.1 Project Team   18
3.3.2 Consultants   19
3.3.3 Departmental IT Security Officer/Audit   19
3.4   Timing   19

4. Implementation 21

4.1	Procedures	22
4.1.1	IT Infrastructure	23
4.1.2	Environment	30
4.1.3	Personnel	33
4.1.4	IT Infrastructure Management	34
4.1.5	Operating Procedures at the New Site	35
4.1.6	Security	36
4.1.7	Transport	37
4.1.8	Contingency Plan - Acceptance	38
4.1.9	Return to Normal	38
4.2	Dependencies	39
4.2.1	Service Level Agreements	39
4.2.2	General	39
4.2.3	Staff	39
4.3	People	39
4.3.1	Consultants	39
4.3.2	Trade Union (T/U) Side	39
4.3.3	Key Operational Staff - Disaster Teams	40
4.3.4	System Users/Applications Managers	40
4.3.5	Support Staff	41
4.3.6	Office Services	41
4.3.7	Messengers	41
4.4	Timing	41

5. Post Implementation 43

5.1	Procedures	44
5.1.1	Testing the Plan	44
5.1.2	Reviewing the Plan	45
5.1.3	Copies of the Plan	45
5.1.4	Audit	46
5.2	Dependencies	46
5.2.1	Access to the Contingency Site	46
5.2.2	Keeping the Plan Up to Date	46
5.2.3	CP Contracts	46
5.3	People	47
5.3.1	Project Team	47
5.3.2	Disaster Teams - Key Operational Staff	47
5.3.3	Users	47
5.3.4	IT Audit	47
5.4	Timing	47

6.	**Benefits, Costs & Possible Problems**	**49**
6.1	Benefits	49
6.2	Costs	49
6.3	Possible Problems	50
6.3.1	Staff Availability	50
6.3.2	Finance	50
7.	**Tools**	**51**
7.1	Preliminary / Planning Stage	51
7.1.1	Project Management	51
7.1.2	Risk Assessment and Management	51
7.1.3	Capacity Planning	51
7.1.4	Network Modelling	51
7.2	Contingency Plan Production	51
8.	**Conclusions & Recommendations**	**53**
9.	**Further Information**	**55**
10.	**Bibliography**	**57**
Annex A.	**Proforma Contingency Plan**	**A-1**
Annex B.	**CRAMM Overview**	**B-1**
Annex C.	**Example Terms of Reference - Preliminary Stage**	**C-1**
Annex D.	**Investment Appraisal for Contingency Planning Measures**	**D-1**

Other modules on IT Infrastructure Management in this series.

Preface

Welcome to the IT Infrastructure Library **Contingency Planning** *module.*

In their respective subject areas, the IT Infrastructure Library publications complement and provide more detail than the IS Guides.

The ethos behind the development of the IT Infrastructure Library is the recognition that organizations are becoming increasingly dependent on IT in order to satisfy their corporate aims and meet their business needs. This growing dependency leads to a growing requirement for high-quality IT services. Quality means 'matched to business needs and user requirements as these evolve'.

This module is one of a series of codes of practice intended to facilitate the quality management of IT Services, and of the IT Infrastructure. (By IT Infrastructure, we mean organizations' computers and networks - hardware, software and computer-related telecommunications, upon which applications systems and IT services are built and run). The codes of practice will assist organizations to provide quality IT service in the face of skill shortages, system complexity, rapid change, current and future user requirements, growing user expectations, etc.

Underpinning the IT Infrastructure is the Environmental Infrastructure upon which it is built. Environmental topics are covered in a separate set of guides within the IT Infrastructure Library. Details of these are available from the CCTA Library Rosebery Court.

IT Infrastructure Management is a complex subject which for presentational and practical reasons has been broken down within the IT Infrastructure Library into a series of modules. A complete list of current and planned modules is available from the CCTA IT Infrastructure Management Services (see Section 9).

Each IT Infrastructure Management module is structured in essentially the same way. There is a Synopsis aimed at Senior Managers (Directors of IT and above, typically down to Civil Service grade 5); a Management Summary aimed at Senior IT people and in some cases 'customers' (typically Civil Service grades 5 - 7); the main body of the text aimed at IT middle management (typically grades 7 to HEO); and technical detail in Annexes.

*Each module contains **guidance** in Sections 3 to 5; **benefits, costs and possible problems** in Section 6, which may be of interest to senior staff; **tools** (requirements and examples of real-life availability) in Section 7; and **conclusions and recommendations**, also of potential interest to senior staff, in section 8.*

CCTA is working with the IT trade to foster the development of software tools to underpin the guidance contained within the codes of practice (ie to make adherence to the module more practicable), and ultimately to automate functions.

If you have any comments on this or other modules, do please let us know. A comment sheet is provided with every module; please feel free to photocopy it or to let us have your views via any other medium.

Thank you. We hope you find this module useful.

Synopsis

As Government Departments' dependency on IT grows, the consequences of a loss of their IT facilities as a result of some 'disaster' are becoming more serious.

To protect against prolonged loss of essential IT facilities, Departments should develop Contingency Plans. This module guides Departments through the process of developing a Contingency Plan. The module includes a proforma plan which Departments can use as a basis for tailoring their own Contingency Plans. The module recommends that, before starting work on a Contingency Plan, Departments use the CCTA Risk Analysis Management Methodology (CRAMM) to analyse the risks to their IT facilities.

1. Management Summary

1.1 If It's Not Worth Protecting It's Not Worth Doing!

This statement may appear rather glib, but it is worthy of consideration. If your IT processing does not have a Contingency Plan, is the processing really necessary at all?

1.2 "It Won't Happen To Me"

Too many managers are content to think of Contingency Planning (CP) as something that would be nice if only they had the time or money. Although there is no routine central recording of disasters in Departments, CCTA have records of 5 major IT disasters in Government during the period 1985-1987. These disasters resulted in serious interruptions to the Departments' business because the Departments had no contingency plans.

1.3 Why Do Contingency Planning?

Departments are increasingly dependent on their IT systems. Their entire business is becoming irrevocably linked to the availability of IT services. To protect the business of state, Departments must therefore:

*   assess the effects of losing their IT services

*   identify critical services and applications that must be maintained

*   identify timescales within which service must be restarted

*   identify means of maintaining/restoring service

*   produce a contingency plan in sufficient detail to enable them to cope with/recover from an IT contingency.

The potential impact of not planning adequately for contingency can range from loss of revenue, through political embarrassment, to loss of service to the public.

1.4 How Does This Module Help?

This module of the IT Infrastructure Library is a comprehensive guide to producing a contingency plan and recovering from a disaster.

It will facilitate:

*   analysis of the most suitable ways of safeguarding the present system

*   replacing the system if disaster strikes.

The module addresses the needs of all classes of IT system including networked and distributed systems. It stresses the importance of planning for contingency to reflect Departments' growing dependence on IT.

1.5 Structure of Module

The main guidance in this module is contained in sections 3 to 5, which address Planning, Implementation and Post Implementation respectively.

The Planning section describes a Preliminary Stage to analyse the risks to Departments' IT facilities using the CCTA Risk Analysis Management Methodology (CRAMM), to consider production of a plan, to get management approval for financing and staffing a CP project and to define terms of reference for it. It also describes the Contingency Options available and the processes of setting up a project team.

The Implementation section covers the development of a contingency plan. When completed the plan will contain all the information needed to recover the IT service in a disaster situation. The plan will also give clear guidance on how and when it should be invoked. It is strongly recommended that you read the guidance given in the module before attempting to complete the proforma contingency plan at Annex A.

The execution of the actions from the Preliminary Stage and the putting in place of measures to underpin the contingency plan (eg off site storage, contracts with CP suppliers) results in the introduction of contingency/resilience measures. These will in many cases prevent an incident becoming a disaster, and reduce the impact of an actual disaster.

The Post Implementation section deals with testing and reviewing the plan.

Emphasis has been placed on giving practical, well tested advice and to this end a proforma plan is appended as Annex A. It is intended that this proforma plan can be used by any Department as the basis for developing its own detailed Contingency Plan.

2. Introduction

2.1 Target Readership

The contents of this module are aimed at Directors of IT, IT Services Managers and at those officers who are tasked with doing risk management and contingency planning.

2.2 Scope

This module deals with planning to cope with, and recover from, an IT disaster (ie loss of service for protracted periods, which requires that work is moved to an alternative system in a non-routine way). It also gives guidance on safeguarding the existing system ie preventing incidents from becoming disasters. The module does not include specific countermeasures to industrial action as this needs to be handled quite differently. The guidance as proposed is not naturally applicable to industrial action as the goodwill and cooperation of staff and suppliers, a prerequisite for ordinary CP, cannot be relied upon in such circumstances.

This module does not go into great detail on assessing risks but recommends that Departments use CRAMM (CCTA Risk Analysis Management Methodology). CRAMM is a complete package which comprises documentation, training and a software support tool and has been designed to be used by IT, but not necessarily IT security, specialists. The package currently caters for systems which process unclassified but sensitive information. Departments with classified information should contact their CCTA Departmental Project Support Officer in CT1 Division at Riverwalk House for advice on risk analysis and management. The Civil Service College is running courses on CRAMM. Further details on CRAMM are available at Annex B, and from the CCTA IT Security and Privacy Group at Riverwalk House.

Note: As it is Government policy not to insure, there are no references to insurance in this document.

2.3 Context

This module is one of a series of guides issued as part of the IT Infrastructure Library. Although this module can be read in isolation, it should be used in conjunction with other modules in the series. Section 2.4 lists the other modules that are most relevant.

The IT Infrastructure Library embodies a systematic approach to the management of the IT infrastructure which will contribute towards the provision of quality IT services. CP is recognized as a key aspect of IT Infrastructure management - needed to maintain a quality service, with minimum 'hiccup', in the event of an IT disaster.

This module replaces the information on CP contained in the following CCTA publications:

*   A guide to Contingency Planning for simple IT systems - in the series, IT in the Civil Service

*   Expenditure on Contingency Planning for computers - IT Circular No 245.

The CCTA recommendation that Departments should use the NCC publication entitled Contingency Planning Today - State of the Art Report by Roger Doswell (recommended as a replacement for CGRS16 (see IT Circular No 283)) is now withdrawn and is replaced by this module

2.4 Related Guidance

It would be advisable to read all of the modules listed below. However, they have been categorised into 3 groups according to the amount of information relevant to this module.

Large amount of relevant information

Service Level Management - gives guidance on the inclusion of modified service levels into Service Level Agreements (SLAs), to apply when a contingency service is in operation. Service Level Management must be continued on the contingency service to ensure service quality is maintained.

Change Management - the Contingency Plan is subject to the Department's normal change control procedures. Change Management must be continued following a move to a contingency site.

Network Management - gives advice on Network Planning, which can be carried out in such a way as to reduce the risk of disaster. The module also gives advice on sizing networks, which may be relevant to providing an emergency service in a contingency situation.

Availability Management - contains information on managing the risk of individual component failure, and on maintaining high levels of availability. These practices can be used to provide 'resilience to disaster'. Availability Management is relevant at the home and contingency site.

Capacity Management - gives guidance to enable sizing of a replacement system to process a Department's critical applications. The module will also assist in the management of capacity at the contingency site.

Medium amount of relevant information

User Liaison - gives guidance on managing the relationship between IT Services and its Users. The User Liaison function can be made responsible for obtaining from Users information which is needed to produce a contingency plan, and for giving Users relevant information when moving to a contingency site.

Configuration Management - particularly relevant to producing and maintaining the IT Asset Registers.

Small amount of relevant information

Help Desk - provision of a Help desk facility will be required at a contingency site.

Other IT Infrastructure Management modules give guidance on practices, such as Problem Management and Change Management, that must be continued at the contingency site.

2.5 Definitions

Note: There is, as yet, no standard nomenclature used throughout the industry, for CP services. The following definitions of cold and hot start apply to this module.

Cold start - provision of a building, either static or portable, providing electrical supply, environmental control and telecommunications connections, capable of supporting a computer but with no computer equipment supplied - **accommodation only.**

Hot start - provision of computer accommodation, either static or portable, with power, environmental services and telecommunications connections together with a computer and supporting peripherals - **accommodation and equipment.**

Electronic vaulting - the practice of using telecommunications lines to archive data, normally for security and contingency purposes.

IT Services Manager - the person with overall responsibility for IT service quality. Typically his/her peer managers are the Applications Development Managers and the Administration and Finance Manager, and they are all responsible to the Department's Director of IT.

PROMPT - the method adopted within Government for planning, managing and controlling IS projects. It provides guidance on the management components (organization, plans & controls) and on the technical components (end products & the activities needed to produce them).

Acronyms and abbreviations used in this module

BT	British Telecom
CCTA	Central Computer and Telecommunications Agency
CP	Contingency planning
CRAMM	CCTA Risk Analysis and Management Methodology
EIFIT	Environmental Infrastructure for IT
IT	Information Technology
I/O	Input/Output
JCL	Job Control Language
LAN	Local Area Network
PC	Personal Computer
PES	Public Expenditure Survey
PROMPT	Project Resource Organization Management and Planning Techniques
PSA	Property Services Agency
PSS	Packet Switch Stream
SLA	Service Level Agreement
TP	Transaction Processing
T/U	Trade Union

2.6 The Need for Contingency Planning

With Government Departments' growing dependency on IT, it is important for them to have IT services that are consistently delivered to an agreed level of quality. Every time the service is unavailable many Departments are unable to carry on running the business of state because there is no practical fallback. This trend towards dependency on IT will continue and will increasingly affect Departments' business managers and policy makers.

It is important, therefore, that Departments assess the effects of losing the use of their IT systems. The loss will vary in cost and inconvenience with the duration of the outage and the criticality of the application or service. But in general Departments will find that they cannot satisfactorily carry on for long without their IT systems.

It is imperative therefore that Departments produce a Contingency Plan which must contain sufficient detail to ensure appropriate actions can be taken to recover the service following a disaster.

2.7 Statistics on Disasters

No official institution in the UK collects statistics on computer disasters. However BIS Applied Systems produce a "Computer Disaster Casebook" which documents over 175 cases of computer disasters.

An analysis of these disasters gives the following breakdown by cause.

**Figure 1:
Causes of Disaster**

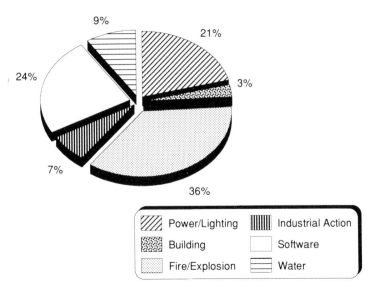

To deal effectively with these risks requires:

*   preventative measures (eg physical security measures, fire detection systems)

*   provision of alternative arrangements (eg standby generators, alternative processing facilities)

*   recovery facilities (eg cleaning equipment).

This module concentrates on planning the use of alternative arrangements. The module gives limited advice on recovery. CRAMM deals with risk countermeasures including prevention.

2.8 Management and Departmental Commitment

Vital as they are, it is important that IT contingency plans are not produced in isolation. There need to be clearly defined interfaces to Departmental contingency plans. For instance, there may be little use in providing a spare computer site for an office automation system which is located on the same premises as its users unless some provision is also made for the users.

It is interesting to note that further analysis of the statistics given in 2.7 shows that 59% of the computer disasters through fire started outside the computer room. This surely shows that IT contingency cannot be considered in "splendid isolation".

There is little doubt that CP requires a good deal of time, effort and possibly cost. It can sometimes be difficult for management to see what exactly it gets for this investment. However, if the incentive of the risk analysis and cost justification exercise is not enough, Departments will also need to be aware of the National Audit Office report entitled Computer Security in Government Departments, published in 1988, which severely criticised them for their lack of Contingency Plans and effective stand-by arrangements.

However Departmental Management comes to realize the importance of CP, its commitment to it is essential. It is strongly recommended that the requirement for CP is agreed at Departmental 'board level' and that the 'board' is informed of progress in developing and testing the plan.

To ensure management commitment CCTA advise that the Director of IT, the IT Services Manager, Service Level Managers and senior User Managers sign a statement, at least annually, to acknowledge they are:

*   content with the Contingency Plan

*   satisfied that it has been adequately tested

*   confident it would work in practice.

This concentrates senior management's attention on CP and helps ensure regular testing is carried out.

3. Planning: The Preliminary Stage

This section of the module describes a Preliminary Stage which results in a report to Management. The report will contain an assessment of the risks to, and vulnerabilities of, a system; an indication of the criticality of applications; and costed options for replacing the service following a disaster. This section also describes the contingency options available and the processes of setting up a project team to produce a Contingency Plan. There is limited information, passim, on preventing disasters but more detailed information is contained in CRAMM.

Preventing disaster in the first place is vital but must not hold up progress on a CP project. Do not allow resources to be diverted into lengthy projects to improve protection whilst neglecting progress on the plan. Many CP projects founder because the initial security review reveals too many problems. The CP team must press ahead with their CP whilst identifying action for IT management and environmental services (eg PSA) which will improve protection.

The end product of this stage is management's approval to develop a Contingency Plan using agreed standby options.

The diagram at Figure 2 is a pictorial representation of the processes involved in the Preliminary Stage.

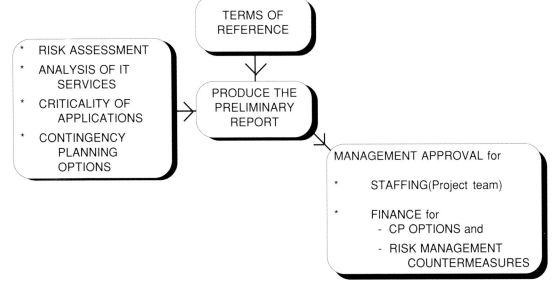

Figure 2: The Preliminary Stage

3.1 Procedures

3.1.1 IT Strategy

The Department must:

* spell out its intentions with respect to IT CP in its IT Strategy Plan

* interface the IT Contingency Plan with Departmental Contingency Plans.

3.1.2 Preliminary Stage: Terms of Reference

Agree definitive terms of reference for each stage of CP (ie Planning, Implementation and Post Implementation as described in sections 3, 4 and 5 of this module), to specify:

* the purpose of the task(s) that constitutes the stage concerned

* who is responsible for completing it(them)

* the resources available to them

* the information which must be available as input to the task(s)

* the end product

* the timescale for completion.

Where the work to be done impacts significantly upon the workload of other parts of the Department, involve the managers of those areas to ensure the resource is made available.

Example terms of reference for the Preliminary Stage are given in Annex C - see also 3.1.3.

3.1.3 Preliminary Stage

Carry out a Preliminary Stage to report to management the need to produce a Contingency Plan, the manpower and other resources needed to do it and the estimated cost of, and timescale for, doing it.

Include in the Preliminary Stage an analysis of perceived risks to the Department's IT service(s) and recommendations as to how these risks should be managed. (CRAMM itemizes all the vulnerabilities of an IT system and the threats to which it is likely to be exposed, and provides options for countering them based on the level of protection required. See 7.1.2 and Annex B.)

Include the following types of threats:

* damage by fire, water and natural disaster

* wilful damage and theft

* system software, hardware, power and environmental failure.

The countermeasures produced from a CRAMM exercise will be numerous and system specific. However the basics for disaster prevention are fairly standard and include:

* good access control procedures

* good fire detection and suppression procedures

* good data and software security procedures

* good procedures to deal efficiently with cases where staff are dismissed for any reason

* good housekeeping practices (eg maintenance of environmental control equipment).

Nevertheless, disaster may strike and CRAMM will recommend CP as a countermeasure against the risk. Therefore, ensure the following activities are carried out in the Preliminary Stage:

* an analysis of the services provided eg. batch, TP, Office etc, which should be available from Service Level Agreements (see the module on Service Level Management)

* an assessment of the criticality of each application run on those services and the delay in processing which each application will tolerate.

In assessing criticality of applications, categorize applications according to their priority eg:

* must be supported within n hours

* must be supported within n days

* not critical.

If certain systems are deemed not to be critical, it is possible to provide an emergency service on a machine which is smaller than the normal one, also possibly supporting a smaller network. However, do not allow any reduction in capacity to compromise the satisfactory performance of any Service Level Agreement (SLA) currently in existence without negotiating with the users modified service levels for contingencies. (These modified service levels may have to be decided iteratively after looking at the costs of various contingency options for alternative processing in the event of disaster). Note that predicting the hardware requirements in such a case can be facilitated by the use of tools available for computer and network capacity planning/modelling (see the IT Infrastructure Library modules on Service Level Management, Capacity Management and Network Management). Note also that the flexibility of being able to use a smaller hardware configuration, often broadens the options open to a Department.

Ensure the Preliminary Stage details:

* a financial appraisal of the proposed CP countermeasures justified by CRAMM (see Annex D)

* alternative methods of providing a range of potentially acceptable service levels, referring, where applicable, to specific commercial service providers and the services they provide (see 3.1.4: some information on commercial services is available from the CCTA contact given in section 9)

* the benefits/disadvantages of using particular options, including their relative costs - see 3.1.4 for information on options available

* the size of CP project team and manpower required.

Present a report to management with recommendations on the course of action to be adopted.

3.1.4 Contingency Options   Consider from the following options available to Departments how best to protect the service, or to replace it on a temporary basis before restoring a permanent service:

* do nothing

* clerical backup procedures

* reciprocal arrangement

* the "fortress" approach

* "cold" start fixed centre

* "cold" start portable centre

* "hot" start - external

* "hot" start - internal

* mobile hot start or "computer on the back of a lorry".

.1 Do nothing

There are few, if any, Departments that can justifiably adopt this option. In the main those that do, work on the mistaken premise that it can never happen to them. This head-in-the-sand attitude may appear attractive financially, in the short term, but any Department that is able to function effectively without its IT services for a long period of time must query whether it needs them at all.

.2 Clerical backup procedures

This option is not feasible in most cases as insufficient staff numbers and skills are available to provide a full clerical system. However, a clerical solution may be feasible for some applications. Note that many contingency plans will include an element of clerical backup procedures and this may reduce the overall IT contingency requirement.

.3 Reciprocal arrangement

This option is typically used when 2 organizations running on compatible machinery agree that each will provide the other, in an emergency, with part or all of the first's IT resource to run the other's work. This type of agreement works best when the workload at both organizations is batch and the sites run for 1 or, at most, 2 shifts. This enables the 'other' site to run its work during the first site's silent hours.

If this type of arrangement is viable for all, or part, of the workload then both sites must:

*   sign a written agreement specifying the service to be provided including when the service can be used, for how long and in what circumstances

*   agree a change management system that will maintain system compatibility.

With the increase in the number of online transaction processing (TP) and Office Automation systems, use of this option has become much less practicable. These systems are conventionally used by staff who need to access them during normal office hours; time slots overnight or at weekends would not be acceptable. The only way to provide a service would be to ensure that only part of the capacity of each system is used, and/or the host system can run at a degraded level to accommodate the other site's requirements. Even if these obstacles could be overcome regular testing and stringent intersite change management must be carried out.

.4 The "fortress" approach

Some organizations adopt a fortress-like approach to CP. This means that they do not have an alternative site to move to, with the financial and logistical problems that that entails. However, money is spent on making the home site as disaster-proof as possible, with lots of built-in redundancy in the computer equipment, high-quality environmental controls, and physical security.

The aim of this approach is to reduce, as far as possible, the risks to the continued provision of the IT service. However well planned it is, it never totally eliminates the possibility of a major disaster occurring. It is impossible to protect a single site from all possible disasters.

.5 "Cold" Start - fixed centre

Cold Start fixed centre describes a service which provides an empty computer room on a fixed site. The room will be equipped with the necessary power, environmental control and telecommunications connections. The user of the service pays an annual subscription for which he has access to the centre for a predetermined length of time in agreed emergency situations.

A separate arrangement needs to be made to acquire the necessary hardware to run at the cold start centre. Suppliers rarely guarantee to supply replacement equipment within a fixed deadline, but normally make their best endeavours to do so.

The advantage to the user of this service is that access should be available to the site almost immediately.

The disadvantages are that:

*   there are very few companies offering this type of service and therefore the chances of such a site being nearby are small

*   such agreements tend to allow occupancy of the site for only a limited period

*   there can be a delay in obtaining replacement equipment

*   there are often difficulties setting up adequate network facilities.

Departments should satisfy themselves that the supplier has the ability to deal with a double hit (ie 2 subscribers needing the facility at the same time). Reputable suppliers lessen the likelihood by limiting the number of subscribers to the service.

.6 "Cold" Start - portable centre This service again relates to the supply of an empty computer room with full power, environmental controls and telecommunications connections. The difference between this and the previous option is that the accommodation is portable and is erected at a site prearranged with the subscriber, normally the car park. If the car park is not usable, eg it is full of debris, the user can nominate a reserve site. The suitability of the site will have been approved by a site survey carried out previously by the contractor. (Departments must check with their local authority and/or cold start contractor whether planning permission must be obtained before this option can be adopted.) The amount of accommodation provided is tailored to the size of the configuration required.

The advantage of this service is that, space permitting, the portable building can be erected adjacent to the home site.

Potential disadvantage lies in the need to provide a suitable secure location near the office and the time taken to erect and commission the building, which can vary from 3 to 10 days depending on the size.

It is important to arrange for the telecommunications provider to provide a secure external telecommunications node at the prearranged standby site, which must be far enough away from the existing site to minimise any threat that could affect both the home site and the standby node (eg put it at the end of the car park furthest from the building).

.7 "Hot" Start - external This service covers the provision of access to a computer hall containing a hardware configuration fully compatible with the Department's needs. Some Departmental IT Divisions cannot afford to finance an exclusive hot-start site. There are, however, a number of commercial companies which provide hot start and spread the cost across a number of subscribers.

The cost varies depending on:

* size of processor(s) needed

* the number and type of peripherals needed

* the software inventory

* the length of time the facility is required.

The obvious advantage of this service is that the customer can have virtually instantaneous access to an operational and fully-tested system, housed in a secure building.

Potential disadvantages are:

* the site is almost certainly some distance from the home site, which presents a number of logistical problems

* annual subscriptions are comparatively expensive and some companies impose an additional daily fee for use of the service in an emergency.

As with fixed cold-start centres, Departments should satisfy themselves that the supplier is able to handle a "double hit", if necessary.

It is important to note that a commercial hot-start agreement limits access to a predetermined length of time, typically a maximum of 16 weeks. This limitation is why many subscribers to hot start also subscribe to a portable cold-start centre.

.8 "Hot" Start - internal

Departments have the option of providing their own hot start internally.

Contingency for single central site / star network infrastructures can be provided by setting up duplicate facilities, each able to process the full workload using the same system software. The contingency centre can be used for systems development, testing and training when not required for emergency processing. It must be situated away from the main centre with any telecommunications supplied through a different exchange. There is no need for special operator training. This form of internal arrangement provides 100% contingency with minimum disruption, but at a price.

Departments with distributed systems, consider providing contingency by leaving spare capacity on all, or some, of the system nodes. Under normal circumstances this spare capacity can be used for development, training or testing, but could be made available quickly when a contingency situation arises at another node.

But CAUTION! Development can be a critical activity that must not be jeopardized to make way for internal standby.

.9 Mobile hot start

"computer on the back of a lorry"

This service is exactly what it says. A company contracts to deliver an agreed system to the customer's site, within a certain time. The machine is contained within a trailer and is transported to the site by a lorry. The trailer is fitted out as a computer room with the necessary environmental services. The Department needs to provide a flat, secure area on which the trailer can be parked. Electricity supply and telecommunications links are probably required from the site to the trailer.

As with all the options it has potential advantages and disadvantages. The advantages are:

*   the companies can offer a quick response to a call for help (eg hours rather than days)

*   the trailer can be installed close to the office.

The disadvantages are:

*   only a very limited number of hardware types are covered commercially by this type of service

*   there are some siting charges if the service is called out

*   special measures may need to be taken to make the site secure.

As with the portable "cold" centre, make provision for a secure external telecommunications node.

.10 Access to contingency site for testing

In all cases where moving to a contingency site is the preferred option, Departments must ensure their contract allows regular access to the site for testing.

3.1.5 Dormant Contracts

Consider speeding up the return to normal operation by setting up dormant contracts. This is a novel concept, which as yet has not been used in Government, to help speed up the process of ordering replacement hardware in emergency situations.

The idea is that a Department will draw up a contract for the supply of hardware which the company would supply only if authorised by the Department to do so. The contract would run for a specified period, say a year, and would have to be renegotiated at the end of that period. This would allow the Department to include any new equipment that had been purchased in the meantime.

The contract could then be activated immediately thus shortening the delivery time. There would obviously be a small annual staff cost incurred in keeping the contract up to date but this would be the only cost to the Department.

3.1.6 Management Approval to Proceed

Submit the Preliminary Stage report to Management for approval of the contingency option proposed and the necessary funds and staffing to produce the Contingency Plan. Draw up terms of reference for the next phase of the operation (see 3.1.2).

3.1.7 Set Up the Project Team

Once the terms of reference for the next phase have been clearly defined and the resources agreed, make the formal allocation of duties. Nominate a CP Manager to be responsible for control of the project, and to chair the project meetings. Brief members of the team who are assigned to the project on their new responsibilities. Whether internal staff or consultants are used, draw up detailed job descriptions. Clearly show the target dates for completing parts or all of the plan. See 3.3.1 for more detailed information on makeup of the team.

3.1.8 Project Management

Control the production of both the Preliminary Stage report and the Contingency Plan, and execution of associated tasks, using a management method such as PROMPT, where the size of the task justifies it.

In any event hold project meetings regularly to ensure control and to review the progress made.

3.2 Dependencies

IT Divisions need management commitment to CP. The IT Strategy should make clear the importance of CP to the maintenance of IT service and hence to the assured running of the Department's business.

Departments need to be aware of the contingency options available and their limitations (see 3.1.4). For further details refer to the CCTA contact shown in Section 9.

3.3 People

3.3.1 Project Team

Assign this team overall responsibility for CP. It will control the production and implementation of contingency plans and be responsible for placing underpinning contracts.

Ensure the team is chaired by the CP Manager and comprises officers representing IT Services Management, including the Service Level Manager; Applications and User Management; administration and finance; and has the power to co-opt other sources of expert advice and opinion as is deemed necessary, eg.

* capacity planners

* network planners

* office services

* auditors

* security officers

* procurement and contracts officers.

3.3.2 Consultants

Departments may consider recruitment of consultants to produce the Preliminary Stage report or the Contingency Plan. However, the use of the proforma plan and CRAMM considerably assists existing staff to carry out this work, with the added benefits that:

* the staff should already know what the organization does and how it does it

* they should be totally independent of industry connections and influences

* they provide continuity and a continued presence after implementation of the plan.

Decide after all these considerations whether a consultancy is needed; if so seek the advice and recommendation of the head of CCTA's Services Industry Support Branch at Riverwalk House on the capabilities and suitability of particular consultancies.

3.3.3 Departmental IT Security Officer/Audit

Consult the Departmental IT Security Officer and Audit and keep them informed of all decisions taken in support of CP, to ensure adherence to physical and logical security standards.

3.4 Timing

Carry out a Preliminary Stage, preferably including a CRAMM review, before producing a Contingency Plan. For new systems, plan for contingency at the outset. For existing systems, if you have not done so already do it now before it is too late.

Base your timetable for the Preliminary Stage on:

* the complexity of the IT system for which the contingency plan is being developed

* the number of services and applications run on it and the number of Users to be interviewed

* the availability and experience of staff

* their knowledge and familiarity with tools eg CRAMM, PROMPT etc

* the availability and quality of consultants, if used

* the speed of response by management and the Departmental IT Security Officer and / or Audit to proposals made.

As each Department's (or installation's) circumstances differ it is impossible to predict a typical timescale.

4. Implementation

The Implementation section covers the development of a contingency plan. When completed the plan will contain all the information needed to recover the IT service in a disaster situation. The plan will also give clear guidance on how and when it should be invoked. Read the guidance given in the module before attempting to complete the proforma contingency plan at Annex A.

If you are designing systems - application systems or IT infrastructures - we suggest you consider the guidance given in this module carefully and design to protect against (or minimize the impact of) disaster. The guidance on coping with disaster should it happen, should be used to shape your CP.

The diagram at Figure 3 is a pictorial representation of the processes involved in the Implementation Stage.

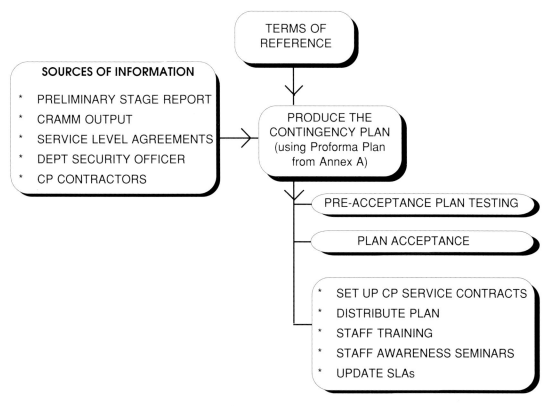

Figure 3: The Implementation Stage

4.1 Procedures

Designate the following responsibilities:

* the CP Manager is the head of the Project Team and will be responsible for the actions of the team

* the Project Team is responsible for producing the plan, which must contain all the information required to recover the agreed level of service in the event of a contingency.

In drawing up the contingency plan, the CP Team should address the items covered in sections 4.1.1 to 4.1.7. In these sections advice is given on protection against disaster, as well as planning to cope if disaster should strike.

In researching and developing the plan, the Team should make use of one of the tools now available. We recommend that Departments use the proforma plan given in Annex A. Some Departments may wish in addition, or instead, to use a commercially available package. Limited information on available tools can be obtained from the contact shown in section 9.

Call upon the following areas of the organization to supply information on:

* emergency services - Administration

* local environment aspects - Administration

* health and safety - Admin/Safety Officer

* staff well-being - Admin/Welfare/Trade Unions

* security - Departmental IT Security Officer

* service and workload priorities - Service Level Manager, User Managers

* program running - Applications managers

* operating instructions - Operations

* contracts - internal

> - Contracts Branch
> CT5 Division of CCTA, Norwich.

As well as producing the plan the Team should accept responsibility for setting up any contracts with contingency service providers and/or other Departments.

4.1.1 IT Infrastructure

.1 Hardware

Note that there are 2 main causes of interruption to service due to hardware failure:

*   breakdown of individual components

*   total loss of the system in a disaster situation.

Guidance to Departments on ways of reducing the risk (and the impact on the system as a whole) of a breakdown of individual components is given in the module on Availability Management. This CP module is concerned with recovering from and coping with a total loss. Note however, that these 'causes' represent 2 extremes on a continuum of 'severity of impact'. Thus, for example, some of the material in the Availability Management module concerned with resilience may be relevant to the prevention of disasters (or, at least, to the prevention of failures becoming 'disasters').

Note that there are a number of standby options open to Departments to recover their service following a disaster: see 3.1.4.

Careful consideration of the way in which the hardware is configured can help Departments' CP. For example a number of large ICL mainframes have dual processors, which can be located up to 1.5Km apart using fibre optic connections; by locating nodes in separate buildings, Departments can provide a degree of 'resilience to disaster'. Where there is a choice Departments may find that dual or multi processors configured in this way are more disaster proof than equivalently powered single processors.

Hardware can become contaminated by exposure to water, smoke, dust etc either directly or indirectly eg through the air conditioning system. In these circumstances approach the manufacturer/maintainer and/or a specialist cleaning company to see whether cleaning is a viable proposition. Invoke the departmental contingency plan to operate, if necessary, while the cleaning work is being undertaken. (It is also likely that the company that maintains the equipment will want to ensure that the cleaning process has been completely effective, before resuming the servicing of the contract.)

**.2 Terminal-based systems
(see also telecommunications
networks)**

Plan for contingency at the same time as your Department
plans its online systems. Conduct a risk analysis exercise, such
as CRAMM, to produce justified countermeasures (as stated in
3.1.3).

Plan for the following occurrences:

* loss of central processing

* loss of cluster controller

* loss of individual terminals.

If there is a loss of central processing for any length of time
over a pre-specified threshold, or if it is clear that the threshold
will be exceeded, invoke the contingency plan as required.
Provide a user service in a number of ways:

* a totally duplicated system at the contingency site - ideal,
   expensive, but possibly cost justifiable

* a more restricted service on a smaller central system, based
   on an analysis of the criticality of the work and managed by
   the introduction of scheduled time slots - cheaper but by no
   means ideal.

Note that most critical processes on an online system are
associated with database access. Consider whether it could be
more economic, or secure, to move some or all of the staff
involved in data entry, at least, to the contingency site for the
length of the outage; there they could use local terminals and
obviate the need for external telecommunication links. Note
that the likely administrative difficulties to be overcome
concern how geographically dispersed the unusable terminals
are, and the willingness of the staff to move.

The loss of a cluster controller will be as problematic as the loss
of central processing to the area served by that controller.
Minimize the problem by geographically distributing the
terminals connected to a cluster controller (eg over different
parts of the site) or by having them switchable, see Figure 4.

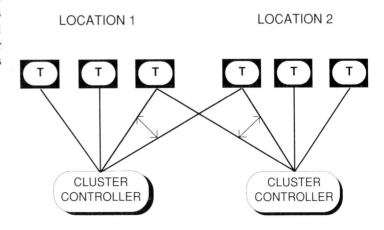

**Figure 4:
Terminals
Distributed
across Cluster
Controllers**

Where there are large distributed systems of cluster controllers, the option is available to provide internal Hot Start at a location nearby, if there is sufficient capacity and geographic distribution.

The loss of individual terminals, which could be disastrous in some circumstances: remedy in one of the following ways:

*   give the user time on a spare terminal nearby

*   move in a spare standby terminal to replace the one that has failed.

The operation of terminal based systems, particularly where the users are not computer literate, is likely to be greatly enhanced by the presence of a Help-desk. This provides a single point for users to direct problems and for those problems to be resolved and answers given. Where a Help-desk is in operation provide in the contingency plan for relocating it, if necessary. See the Help-desk module for more information.

**.3 Telecommunications
Networks**

CP for networks is largely a matter of designing them to be resilient to disaster. In considering CP options for networks take account of any specific system security requirements.

When designing networks, consider the amount of inbuilt
disaster resilience required. The main factors to be taken
account of are:

* the criticality of the services

* whether the services can be provided, at least on a
  temporary basis, without using the network

* the amount of money available to invest in the network.

Plan for the following 2 occurrences with respect to
telecommunication lines:

* loss of all the lines

* loss of individual lines.

Loss of all lines.

This is likely to be as a result of the following:

* loss of an exchange or the 'tail' from the exchange to the
  computer centre

* industrial action at the telecommunications company.

The main supplier of telecommunications lines is BT and it is
normally to BT that Departments go to obtain their services.
Safeguard against loss of an exchange, or the connection to it,
by duplication of lines between separate exchanges where
deemed necessary (see Figure 5) or by setting up alternative

**Figure 5:
Telecomms Lines to
Separate Exchanges**

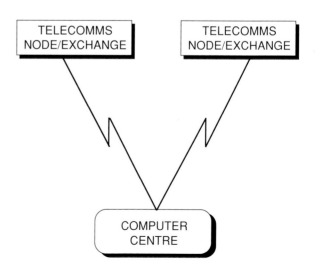

Figure 6:
Telecomms Lines
Duplicated to the
Same Exchange

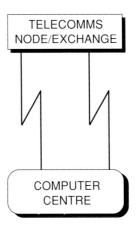

Figure 6:
Telecomms Lines
Duplicated to the
Same Exchange

routes from the building/IT system to the exchange (see Figure 6). Ensure if alternative routing is asked for, that a genuine alternative route is provided and not just another connection through the same channel.

Now that Mercury provide an alternative to BT another means of spreading the risk is by contracting part of the supply to both companies. This advice is particularly relevant if industrial action at the telecommunications company is perceived as a possible threat.

Consider another alternative, of using intelligent terminals for key, or all, nodes. Then, with suitable system design, local processing could continue (albeit probably depleted) with the data being transferred to the central system later.

Loss of individual lines.

Remedy in one of the following ways:

*   invoke a 'dial backup' facility if this is available and the speed/quality is acceptable

*   use an alternative route

*   run affected terminals in local mode recording to another medium which can be input to the system later.

Note that BT's Packet Switch Stream (PSS) facility provides in-built resilience by automatically switching routes, if necessary, once data is in the system.

Special considerations for Local Area Networks

Guard against the possibility of a whole network going down. Departments should consider setting up a number of smaller interconnected networks. Spread the risk and ensure that one problem device cannot corrupt the whole network. Restrict the number of terminals on a LAN to the maximum number of terminals that can be out without the service being seriously impaired.

Although switching to an alternative server in an emergency should be a relatively easy task, ensure clear instructions are available in the operating procedures on how and when to:

* reconfigure the new server

* recreate users' files

* backup files.

.4 Software

Wherever possible use proven systems and applications software; test it as fully as practicable in your environment; safeguard it carefully. When developing applications programs ensure the specification and writing are quality assured, and that acceptance testing is carried out before live running. Almost a quarter of recorded disasters are caused by faults in software: see Figure 7 (2.8 gives details of origin). Faulty software can cause potentially serious interruptions to service and the lack of a regression path to trusted versions can translate these interruptions into disasters.

**Figure 7:
Percentage
of Disasters
Caused by
Software Failure**

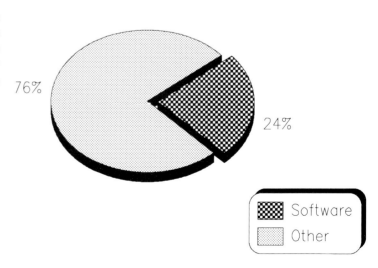

Take copies of each software item and store them at a remote site, together with any related documentation and operating and recovery instructions necessary.

Ensure that software bought or developed by the home site will run at the contingency site. Review and trial regularly, particularly when a new version of the system software is introduced. Details of any problems encountered should be recorded on the incident/action log for the trial, and the causes of the problems resolved. Any resultant tailoring that is needed to enable work to run on the contingency site will be recorded in the job operating instructions.

Ensure, when agreeing terms for the provision of software by an outside supplier, that the licence is valid for use at another site if required. An additional fee may be payable. Similarly it is important to confirm whether any software checks the serial number of the processor before it will operate. In those circumstances it will be necessary to ensure a version is operable at the contingency site.

Maintain an inventory of the software, currently in use, in the Department's Asset Register. For more information on this subject see the Configuration Management module.

.5 Data input/preparation

Because the partial or total loss of a data preparation(dp) unit can be as crippling to Departments that still use them, as the loss of their other IT facilities, consider the CP for both IT and dp facilities together.

As the equipment used in dp tends to be restricted to a few manufacturers, the viable options are greater. These are:

* use of a bureau

* use of a standby or reciprocal site(s) but see 3.1.4 for possible problems with reciprocal arrangements

* splitting the internal facility into more than one area either in the same building or separate buildings if feasible.

It is worth noting that data preparation facilities can be a useful means of preparing and storing data while a central processor is out of action. Users can still submit batch work which is converted to magnetic media for input when the central processor is back online.

If work is to be processed outside the building, take special care to safeguard the security of the data. Similarly if staff are expected to work at a site other than their normal workplace, reach prior agreement with them on transportation, times of attendance, allowances payable etc.

Where necessary arrange alternative means of transporting input and output material, and detail the arrangements in the Contingency Plan.

It is important to keep a secure copy of keying instructions for use in an emergency situation.

.6 Computer stationery and output handling

Make arrangements if special paper handling processes such as bursting, decollating, trimming or enveloping are required. Consider this need; it could influence the choice of contingency site. Alternatively transport the stationery to another site or bureau for processing.

Take account, when planning for contingency, of computer stationery. Store, possibly in the secure media store, sufficient stationery to last until fresh supplies can be obtained. Note that in the case of standard stock items this may be a short lead time, but for special stationery the lead time is likely to be longer. Where such things as blank payable orders or girocheques are involved, make secure arrangements.

4.1.2 Environment

.1 Accommodation

Note that this module does not cover the permanent replacement of general office or computer accommodation.

Departmental contingency plans need to cover the reaccommodation of terminal users should the whole building be destroyed. There is no point in providing replacement computing if there are no users to use it.

Include the temporary office accommodation needs of IT Services staff:

* needed to administer the plan ie an Emergency Control Centre (ECC)

* providing the Operations/data preparation service plus support(engineers, Help Desk etc)

* involved in input/output processing

and of messengers.

Recognize that although it would be ideal, there are likely to be few Departments that can set aside a room exclusively for use as an ECC, from which to control disaster recovery. However designate one inhouse for this purpose with another either in a separate building nearby, or at the contingency site in case the original one has been destroyed or is unusable for any reason. Ensure the ECC is easily accessible, secure and as close as practicable to the affected facility. The ECC must contain copies of the Contingency Plan plus supplies of any other items needed to support the administration of the recovery operation (eg. desks, phones).

Provide sufficient and suitable office accommodation at a contingency site for all officers who are directly providing or supporting the computer/dp operation. Ensure this contains the necessary furniture, equipment, telephones etc. Consider the provision of sleeping accommodation for shift workers particularly if there is limited, or no, accommodation available locally. Consider also the provision of personal hygiene and catering facilities.

For more information on the subject of accommodation refer to the Environmental Infrastructure modules of the IT Infrastructure Library or contact the Head of CCTA's Environmental Infrastructure Services at Riverwalk House.

.2 Power Supply

Note from Figure 8, power and lighting failures account for over 20% of contingencies.

**Figure 8:
Percentage of
Disasters Caused
by Power/Lighting
• Failures**

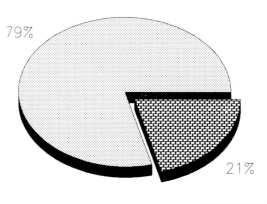

79%

21%

Power/Lighting
Other

Designing power supply to minimize impact of failure

The requirements for prime and backup power supply are obviously an integral part of the design of any new computer accommodation. However requirements do change. Reappraise the quality and security of the supply when significant changes to the load are anticipated. Changes outside the computer area may impact upon the supply to the computer room.

Consider the alternatives available to counter the chance of a break or interruption to the public supply:

* backup generators

* uninterruptible power supplies

* motor alternator sets.

Decide which alternative to choose depending on how critical it is to ensure the supply is unbroken. If the level of backup deemed sufficient does not provide for continuous running, give clear instructions on how to recover the system when the power is restored after an unscheduled break.

Power supply at the backup site

The supply of power at a backup site is likely to be the responsibility of the 'landlord'. However, check the power to ensure that it provides the level and quality needed to support the contingency service.

For more information on the subject of power supply refer to the Environmental Infrastructure modules of the IT Infrastructure Library or contact the Head of CCTA's Environmental Infrastructure Services at Riverwalk House.

.3 Air Conditioning

Designing air conditioning to minimize impact of failure

As with the supply of power, assess the required amount and type of standby air conditioning, where possible, when the accommodation is being designed. If, however, existing accommodation is to be adapted then call in environmental experts to advise on the capacity required and the best way of providing it.

Note that for the purposes of CP it is customary to build in to air conditioning systems sufficient resilience to allow various parts to be repaired, replaced or maintained without seriously affecting the environment. This is sometimes achieved by a mixture of equipment in a central plant room and free-standing units, both with some spare capacity.

A very high level of reliability is increasingly required, and should become the norm. Nevertheless a duplicated plant room is likely still to be too expensive an option. However, consider how an alternative air conditioning supply could be provided quickly in an emergency.

It is quite often a feature of air conditioning systems that if an element fails a reserve is switched in with no discernible interruption. However, provide staff with clear instructions on what action to take, if any, in the event of a failure.

Carry out regular tests of the air conditioning using the standby power supply.

Note that there are now sophisticated Building Management Systems available, capable of both monitoring and automatically adjusting all aspects of the environment. These systems are however quite expensive.

Air conditioning at the backup site

It is important to check before entering into an agreement, particularly where a cold start facility is being used, that the air conditioning at the site is sufficient to cater for the needs of the hardware to be installed.

For more information on the subjects of air conditioning and Building Management Systems refer to the Environmental Infrastructure modules of the IT Infrastructure Library or contact the Head of the CCTA's Environmental Infrastructure Services at Riverwalk House.

4.1.3 Personnel

Identify any skills which are resident in only one person in the organization, and which would be critical if not available during normal operations or in contingency mode. Train other staff in the same skills, or make arrangements for adequate cover (eg consultancy). Document the functions of the individual fully.

Ensure that any staff that are temporarily relocated, as a result of a disaster, should not be inconvenienced financially as a result of agreeing to serve at that other site.

Inform staff fully of their part in carrying out contingency plans.

4.1.4 IT Infrastructure
Management

The disciplines which are used to ensure the smooth provision of quality IT services at the home site must continue on the contingency system. Ensure, therefore, that the management of the IT Infrastructure on the contingency system remains to IT Infrastructure Library standards. However, if contingency arrangements are provided on a reciprocal basis it may not be possible to maintain complete control and it will be necessary for liaison, eg on problem and change management, between the IT Services Teams of both sites. Where contractors are providing contingency facilities, it will generally be necessary to ensure their active participation in IT Infrastructure Management activities and controls.

The Service Level Manager(s) must ensure that Service Level Agreements are adhered to (modified with the consent of User Management, if necessary, to cater for the contingency situation (see 3.1.3)). The Service Level Manager must analyse all aspects of the provided service and its quality and review the results with the User Manager(s). They must agree any action required where shortfalls occur.

The Availability Manager must review the availability achieved and carry out any actions which are deemed necessary, and feasible, to improve the service. This will be done in close liaison with the Service Level, Configuration, Change and Problem Managers and the CP contractor, where applicable.

The Capacity Manager must review performance and recommend any tuning or 'demand management' changes in liaison with the Service Level, Change, Problem and User Managers.

The Security Manager must monitor achievements in the security area and take any corrective/preventative action required.

The Configuration and Change Managers must be fully involved where any changes to the service or the IT Infrastructure are proposed.

The Problem Manager must be fully involved in the analysis and resolution of all problems that occur on the contingency system.

The Help Desk must continue to provide day-to-day support to Users.

Where a service is shared under reciprocal arrangements the IT Services teams from both sites must work together to ensure their respective interests are looked after.

For further information on these activities, please refer to the IT Infrastructure Library modules that address them.

4.1.5 Operating Procedures at the New Site

Recognize that it is often the case that the operations configuration at the contingency site does not mirror that at the home site.

Recognize also that it is probable that the operators will be expected to operate differently from the way they normally do. For instance a number of procedures or practices on the site may be different:

* system loading

* system running

* peripheral handling

* peripheral cleaning

* telecommunications configuration

* media handling including:

    - storage

    - cleaning

    - evaluation

    - library functions

* job priorities

* job identification and presentation

* output handling

* file copying and archiving

* security - see 4.1.6.

Provide the staff who are expected to operate at the contingency site with full written instructions, in advance. Ensure they understand them and have the opportunity to take part in the testing sessions that are held. (Testing the plan is covered in 5.1.1).

4.1.6 Security

Consider a number of different aspects relating to security:

* people

* IT security and audit

* data

* offsite data storage.

When considering the suitability of sites for contingency ensure that the level of physical security is at least as high as at the home site, if not higher.

.1 People

Inform people who are expected to work at the contingency site about the basic security system in operation and the need to respect it. Control access to the building and/or computer area and devise a system for notifying the contingency site of the names of officers who will be attending the site during an emergency. Agree with the contingency site the system of allocating security passes, cardkeys and access numbers.

.2 IT security and audit

The degree of security which is in operation at the home site depends on the sensitivity of the work being done there. Involve the IT Security Officer at all stages of planning to ensure that a sufficiently high level of security is maintained after moving to the contingency site.

The IT Auditor must ensure that the necessary audit trail still exists, and the audit team is able to access the system at the new site by using the appropriate data retrieval and audit packages.

.3 Data - magnetic media

Copy data onto the relevant magnetic media, for security purposes; carry this out in a controlled and regular way to provide adequate backup with which to commence reprocessing quickly.

Ensure that the systems and applications programs, and data files, needed to reconstitute the service, are copied and stored in a secure and controlled environment. Select one offsite for this purpose if possible, but definitely one away from the working copies. If the contingency site is not very far away, consider storing the security copies there. Recognize this would facilitate transfer to the site in an emergency but would require transporting of fresh copies on a regular basis (see below for more details on off site storage).

If fire safes are used to store data, give careful consideration as to where they are sited. Note that in a number of cases the safe has been effective in protecting the media but has itself been rendered inaccessible. Some are not waterproof either! It is also important to keep a duplicate set of safe keys stored securely, away from the site. When storing media in a safe keep a list of what they contain stored with them. This will save valuable time in identifying the contents of the media in an emergency.

.4 Data - online access

Recognize that online access to a shared system, be it at the home or the contingency site, may pose security problems. Protect the security of data by the use of discrete access controls, such as passwords, user login identities, file libraries and data encryption. If required, install dedicated communications lines to maintain confidentiality.

.5 Offsite storage

Ensure the backup storage site provides good physical security and is preferably in a different building. Store any magnetic media in a controlled environment. Ensure that access to the backup is available quickly in an emergency situation.

Recognize that a number of commercial options are open to Departments for the secure storage of data. Banks provide a very secure storage but often access is limited to their normal hours of business and any transporting is the responsibility of the Department. A number of commercial companies now provide services for the collection, storage and delivery of magnetic media and paper records.

Some commercial companies are also thinking about setting up services for the collection and storage of data via electronic vaulting.

Departments considering using these facilities should investigate companies to satisfy themselves of the quality of service provided.

Ensure at the very least the company's security, environmental control and records are as good as those at the Department. A reputable company belongs to a recognised trade association.

4.1.7 Transport

If a number of people have to travel regularly to the contingency site to work consider whether it might be more economic, and better for staff morale, if transport were arranged for them.

Management must ensure that staff are made aware of travel arrangements and allowances payable, and make monies available to reimburse or pay transport bills immediately if required.

Develop plans for the transfer of magnetic media between the secure store and the contingency site. Decide upon a suitable means for input and output material (including post and internal mail) to be transported. Remember that security copying of media must continue after transferring to the contingency site, and that transport of media to a secure site needs to be organized. (Recognize that another site must be available if the contingency site was also the secure site.)

Ensure that instructions on transporting items to and from a contingency site, and who is to do it, are contained in the plan.

If it is intended to use the Departmental messenger services, and the arrangements propose changes to normal duties, consult the staff and T/U Side to agree the revised arrangements.

4.1.8 Contingency Plan - Acceptance

Ensure that the Contingency plan is signed off by senior management after it has been tested (see also section 5).

Following acceptance of the completed plan, the CP team should:

* ensure any contracts are placed

* distribute the plan, ensuring that security copies are stored offsite

* arrange any staff training required

* arrange formal presentations on the contents of the plan to all affected staff

* liaise with Service Level Manager(s) to ensure agreed changes are incorporated in SLAs and to ensure that users are informed about them and understand them

* ensure the plan is regularly tested and revised.

4.1.9 Return to Normal

Plan for the eventual return to the home site, but most of this planning will take place post-disaster and detailed guidance on this is outside the scope of this module.

Recognize, however, that the time taken to return to normal depends on the amount of damage to, and time to replace, any one of the following:

* computer and/or other equipment

* accommodation

* telecommunications lines.

The time taken to return to normal depends also on the schedule of work required to clear up any backlog that has built up. Departments should consider whether it is necessary to process all the backlog or whether certain processes can be waived (eg provision of statistical information, calculation of overpayments).

Decide when and how to return to normal depending on the extent of the disaster, duration of outage and the processing of the backlog. Spend time reviewing the IT Strategy, and capacity planning and service level targets; and decide whether any new management practices should be introduced to prevent a recurrence of the cause of the disaster.

4.2 Dependencies

4.2.1 Service Level Agreements

Include in the Service Level Agreements any agreed relaxation of requirements on the normal service that will be applicable in a contingency situation.

4.2.2 General

To ensure CP works effectively, develop and test plans exhaustively (see 5.1.1), set up all relevant contracts and see they are agreed and understood.

4.2.3 Staff

Ensure the full cooperation and commitment of staff.

4.3 People

4.3.1 Consultants

If consultants are used to complete part, or all, of the plan, monitor their progress regularly, at least once a week. It is also advisable, if consultants have been used to complete the Preliminary Stage, and consultants are also to produce the plan, to use the same ones if possible (provided their previous work was satisfactory). This will reduce the learning curve and therefore reduce the cost of producing the plan.

4.3.2 Trade Union (T/U) Side

Keep the local T/U Side informed of progress throughout the project. In particular consult them where aspects relating to staff and staffing are concerned. To enable successful CP ensure the goodwill and cooperation of the staff.

4.3.3 Key Operational Staff
- Disaster Teams

Key operational staff are those needed to carry out the provisions of the plan. Included here are computer operations, network control, I/O control, data preparation staff and Problem, Change and Configuration Management personnel, ie the ones likely to be most affected by implementing the plan. Consult them about:

* any problems of travelling regularly to another site

* any problems associated with working at that site

* their availability to work different shifts if necessary

* their availability to work unsociable hours including nights or weekends.

Note the implementation of plans has failed in the past because these simple precautions have not been taken.

To make the most productive use of key staff in an emergency they should be organized into disaster teams and given specific areas of responsibility and tasks to perform. Greater detail on the organization and responsibilities of these teams can be found in Annex A 1.3 - 1.4.

Include any training required on unfamiliar equipment in the contract for the replacement service. Consult staff on this matter.

4.3.4 System Users/
Applications Managers

Ensure basic information on the criticality of systems, be they TP, Office Automation, batch or whatever, has been provided by the users at the Preliminary Stage, or is available in Service Level Agreements. For the purposes of developing a plan, require Applications Managers to provide instructions, which are both current and clear, and have been trialled, for running their systems on a contingency service (eg new JCL/SCL, cataloguing/file placement etc).

Ensure the plan contains a mechanism for informing users of any changes required to allow jobs to run at the contingency site; eg different passwords, device identities, etc and of any reductions in the facilities available, to whom and when. Any such reductions should have been incorporated in the Service Level Agreements.

4.3.5 Support Staff

Ensure sufficient support will be given to Users, operations, telecomms etc. either on-site or on call. Note - it is possible that some of these services will be provided by staff from the contingency site.

4.3.6 Office Services

Obtain information relating to buildings, power, telephones and emergency services, at the home and contingency site, from Office Services to help prepare a plan.

4.3.7 Messengers

Ensure that instructions on transporting items to and from a contingency site, and who is to do it, are contained in the plan.

If it is intended to use the Departmental messenger services, and the arrangements propose changes to normal duties, consult the staff and T/U Side to agree the revised arrangements.

4.4 Timing

Recognize that until a Department has a working Contingency Plan they are at risk. This means that Departments which have an IT system without a contingency plan should start work on a plan now. In the case of new systems develop the plan alongside the system itself and make it available as soon as the system goes live, and the Department begins to depend on it. Design new systems with 'resilience to disasters' in mind.

Recognize that the main aim of the Project Team during the implementation phase is to a produce a working contingency plan in accordance with projected timescales and within budget. How effective they are will depend largely on the experience and training of the staff and the tools at their disposal. It is hoped that this module and the proforma plan that accompanies it will improve their effectiveness.

Recognize that some parts of the planning may take a while to achieve, particularly the agreement of any contracts. Start this part of the work as quickly as possible.

When the plan is ready for implementing hold one or more formal presentations or seminars at which the contents of the plan will be presented to all affected departmental staff. Explain the need for a plan, the contingency option(s) adopted and the roles and responsibilities of the staff. Ensure a senior management presence (eg Director of IT) at the presentation to help sell the importance of the plan to the staff.

5. Post Implementation

This section covers testing and reviewing the plan.

The process of plan review and amendment must be an integrated part of the organization's change management system.

As stated in 2.8, to ensure management commitment CCTA advise that the Director of IT, IT Services Manager, Service Level Managers and senior User Managers sign a statement, at least annually, to acknowledge they are:

*   content with the Contingency Plans

*   satisfied that they have been adequately tested

*   confident they would work in practice.

This concentrates senior management's attention on CP and helps ensure regular testing is carried out.

The contents of Figure 9 represent the processes involved in the Post Implementation Stage.

TESTING THE CONTINGENCY PLAN

*   DRY RUNNING

*   PRACTICAL TESTING AT HOME SITE

*   PRACTICAL TESTING AT CONTINGENCY SITE

REVIEW THE CONTINGENCY PLAN

*   CHANGE MANAGEMENT

*   FOLLOWING REGULAR TEST or EVERY SIX MONTHS (whichever is less)

*   AT REVIEW OF SERVICE LEVEL AGREEMENTS

*   AFTER A DISASTER

REVIEW CONTRACTS (with CP Contractors)

*   PART OF CP REVIEW

*   PRIOR TO EXPIRY

*   FOLLOWING ORGANIZATIONAL CHANGE

Figure 9: The Post Implementation Stage

5.1 Procedures

5.1.1 Testing the Plan

Test the plan:

*   when it is first written, before it can be accepted as a working document

*   on a regular basis thereafter, at least annually.

Testing should consist of:

*   dry runs through the plan, or particular parts of it, especially parts that have changed

*   practical tests, using the contingency site (if applicable), with Departmental staff running actual work on the standby IT system.

Testing should be carried out to ensure:

*   the currency of the contents of the plan

*   that the plan is workable

*   the preparedness of the staff.

Although the testing of plans is very important ensure that the processing of live work is not compromised by any test disaster (for example, by choosing carefully who is in the team and by judicious timing of the tests).

Consider the following testing scenarios:

*   unannounced tests

*   random selection of staff (eg stop every fourth member of staff entering the building) to be involved in testing

*   disable major disc or tape volumes (eg bar access to the main media library) to test whether backup facilities are adequate.

Evaluate the success of the tests against predefined criteria (eg how long to restore the service, how many problems and of what severity) and make recommendations to the appropriate level of Departmental or IT Management about changes to the plan, additional staff training etc.

Experience shows that initial testing can go drastically wrong. Be prepared either to abort a test in such circumstances or to let the test continue after noting the problem, and making temporary changes to the plan.

5.1.2 Reviewing the Plan

The Contingency Plan should be reviewed regularly to ensure it is maintained up-to-date; to check that the 'business', user and IT requirements that it addresses are current; to check that the CP staffing requirement is current; to ensure that CP contracts reflect present needs; and to be certain that lessons learnt from tests and any actual disaster have been incorporated.

The CP Manager should ensure that the Project Team reviews the plan regularly, at least every 6 months, in collaboration with User Management; after the annual test; following an actual disaster.

CP reviews should be done at the same time as Service Level Agreement(SLA) reviews. Changes to the Contingency Plan may affect the SLA's, and vice versa.

As part of the organization's change control system the CP Team must:

* assess the impact on the Contingency Plan of all proposed changes to the system

* update the Contingency Plan as and when changes are authorised, and inform everyone who is affected by the update.

5.1.3 Copies of the Plan

Copies of the plan should be stored in the offsite store and Emergency Control Centre ready for use in a disaster situation.

Copies should also be given to:

* Departmental Security Officer

* IT Audit

* Head of IT Services or designated representative

* computer operations

and other areas as appropriate.

It is likely that the plan will contain classified and/or sensitive information, and must therefore be kept secure.

It is imperative that copies of the plan are kept up-to-date. Use of a formalized change management system will assist in this task. If holders of the plan are responsible for updating their copy, we suggest that you audit from time to time to ensure that copies are up to date.

5.1.4 Audit

The CP team's activities should be audited regularly to ensure they conform to the procedures described in this module. The aspects to be checked are self evident from the guidance given in Sections 3 and 4 but will include:

* risk analysis has been carried out and is current (eg has been done in the last 6 months)

* the contingency plan is in conformance with the proforma plan at Annex A

* the plan has been updated in accordance with the Department's change control procedures

* the plan has been tested at regular intervals and the results reported to management

* any underpinning contracts with CP contractors are current

* the annual statement has been signed by management to affirm their confidence in the plan.

5.2 Dependencies

**5.2.1 Access to the
Contingency Site**

Where appropriate there must be access to the contingency site to allow for realistic and effective testing of the plan.

**5.2.2 Keeping the Plan
Up to Date**

The CP Manager is responsible for ensuring the contingency plan is kept up to date. This can only be accomplished if the CP Manager is kept informed of the following:

* information on all IT changes (via the Change Management system)

* other relevant Departmental changes eg accommodation

* IT strategy changes.

5.2.3 CP Contracts

Departments must ensure that contracts entered into, with CP contractors, are current, and continue to reflect the Department's needs. Contracts must be reviewed:

* as part of a CP review

* some months before the contract terminates (to facilitate orderly renewal or cancellation)

* if an organizational change (eg of IT Infrastructure, workload or location) occurs that makes the CP contract inadequate or unsuitable.

5.3 People

This section is a synopsis of the various people involved with CP at the post implementation stage.

5.3.1 Project Team

The team, which may well now be reduced in size, should be given a continuing brief for ensuring that:

* the plan remains workable

* any formal contracts are updated, renegotiated and/or renewed

* the plan reflects the current Departmental strategic planning.

The CP Manager should retain responsibility for the actions of the Team.

5.3.2 Disaster Teams - Key Operational Staff

Ensure that teams, and team members, are kept informed of any changes to the plan which impact upon their responsibilities, and the tasks they are to perform when a contingency arises.

These are the staff most likely to be affected by an impromptu test. They include computer operations, network control and data preparation staff; and also Problem, Change and Configuration Management personnel. These staff are particularly likely to be affected if the test involves moving to the contingency site.

Give due consideration when planning a test to ensure that these staff are given as little inconvenience as possible, thus retaining their morale and motivation.

5.3.3 Users

Running of live work at the home site must not be disrupted without the prior agreement of the Users (and the Service Level Manager).

5.3.4 IT Audit

Involve Audit actively in monitoring how effective the plan is. Ask them to help organize a test strategy, to observe actual tests and report to management. Also give Audit responsibility for the regular audits of the CP function as described in 5.1.4.

5.4 Timing

The time factors involved in testing and reviewing the plan are outlined in 5.1.1 and 5.1.2. Regularly test the plan. How often depends on whether there are significant changes made to it, but do it at least annually. Recognize that the staff turnover rate may affect the frequency of testing. Make good use of any testing time included in contracts with CP service providers.

6. Benefits, Costs & Possible Problems

6.1 Benefits

As Departments become more and more dependent on IT the real costs of not planning for contingencies, and therefore the consequential benefits of doing so, can only be established by carrying out a structured risk analysis. Departments must realise that the risk is to their business and not just their IT systems. By adopting the guidance in this module Departments will reduce the number of breaks and disasters that occur, and reduce the impact of those that do.

In particular, Departments will gain from contingency planning a general reduction of risk to their IT services, and in a disaster:

* the ability to recover the IT system(s) in a controlled manner

* reduction of lost time, providing greater continuity of service to Users

* minimal interruption to the Departments' business.

This module of the IT Infrastructure Library is designed to help Departments make the most efficient and effective use of resources in support of CP. The advice and guidance given should enable any person, however inexperienced, to get up to speed on the subject quickly. It should facilitate the analysis of the most suitable ways of safeguarding the present system and replacing it quickly if disaster strikes.

Also provided in the module is a standardized set of proforma documents which, together with existing site documentation, form the basis of a contingency plan. Each proforma is accompanied by recommended completion instructions. By using them a department can introduce a comprehensive and structured approach to CP and also make optimum use of valuable time and effort.

6.2 Costs

The main overheads incurred in adopting this module are:

* cost and time of producing a contingency plan - could be several man-months for medium-sized systems

* cost of any software package used to help develop a contingency plan

* capital cost of implementing risk management recommendations eg additional equipment - likely to be cheaper if CP is 'designed in' to new systems

* ongoing cost of the replacement option, which will depend on size and other factors - eg hot standby fee is likely to be in the range £5K - £150K, cold standby £4K - £12K

* ongoing cost of maintaining the plan - typically several man-months per annum

* recurring cost of testing and reviewing the plan - typically several man-months per annum.

But can Departments afford not to continue the business of state?

For more information on investment appraisal for CP measures see Annex D.

6.3 Possible Problems

6.3.1 Staff Availability

One possible problem in implementing this Guidance is in resourcing the Project Team. However, when Departments have read this module they will realize how important it is to plan for contingency, and ensure the necessary resource is made available.

A short term problem might arise if the live system is to be kept running whilst the plan is being tested. This situation could increase the number of staff required to cover the 2 operations. However, if all else fails, it may well be possible to test at weekends or public holidays.

6.3.2 Finance

Departments will need to include the costs for CP in their PES and Supply estimates. If the money to do CP adequately is not forthcoming the Department's business is placed at risk.

7. Tools

7.1 Preliminary / Planning Stage

Departments can be helped in the production of the Preliminary Stage report by using available software tools. The aspects where help is available are:

* project management

* risk assessment and management

* capacity planning

* network modelling.

7.1.1 Project Management

Producing a Contingency Plan can be a major project in itself, depending on the size and complexity of the hardware and applications involved. Where the size of the task warrants it PROMPT (Project Management System) must be used to review and control the development of the plan. Further details are available from the head of CCTA's Framework Branch in Gildengate House, Norwich.

7.1.2 Risk Assessment and Management

In the past little assistance was available for carrying out risk assessment and management for IT systems. However CCTA has developed the CRAMM package which now fills this gap. Further details are available at Annex B, and from IT Security and Privacy Group, at Riverwalk House.

7.1.3 Capacity Planning

Capacity Planning tools assist Departments to assess their hardware requirements for contingency purposes. For further details see the IT Infrastructure Library Capacity Management module.

7.1.4 Network Modelling

Network modelling tools assist Departments in designing a network to meet their contingency requirements. For details see the IT Infrastructure Library Network Management module.

7.2 Contingency Plan Production

There are a small number of tools on the market which provide the user with a proforma plan. The majority of them have been developed in the US and have had little adaptation for the UK market. CCTA has produced a paper proforma plan which is tailored for the Government user. This is attached at Annex A.

8. Conclusions & Recommendations

Departments are at risk from disasters and must lay plans to guard against them, particularly as they become more and more IT dependent. They should follow the three stages explained in sections 3, 4 and 5 of this module. These are:

* Planning - Carry out a Preliminary Stage, preferably using CRAMM, to assess what countermeasures are justified

* Implementation - Produce a Contingency Plan

* Post-Implementation - Review, revise and test the plan regularly.

CCTA strongly recommends that Departments ensure management commitment by getting the Director of IT, IT Services Manager, Service Level Managers and senior User Managers to sign a statement, at least annually, to acknowledge they are:

* content with the Contingency Plans

* satisfied that they have been adequately tested

* confident they would work in practice.

This concentrates senior management's attention on CP and helps ensure regular testing is carried out.

9. Further Information

For further information on the contents of this module contact:

IT Infrastructure Management Services
CCTA
Gildengate House
Upper Green Lane
Norwich
NR3 1DW

Telephone: 0603-694788   (GTN: 3014-4788)

10. Bibliography

Dr KK Wong and WF Farquhar. *Computer Disaster Casebook.*
London: BIS Applied Systems Ltd, 1987.

Annex A. Proforma Contingency Plan

Preface

This plan contains the information needed to restore an IT service following a disaster at [insert location].

The plan is laid out in such a way that it should be easy to use in an emergency situation to facilitate initial recovery, and a controlled return of the IT service and customer service to normal.

An A4-size loose-leaf version of the proforma plan is separately available from CCTA.

Plan Updating

It is imperative that the plan is kept up to date. The Contingency Planning(CP) Manager is responsible for ensuring this by arranging regular review meetings and through formal change management procedures. More information on these subjects is available in the IT Infrastructure Library module on change management.

Amended pages or sections of the plan will be distributed to officers who have a copy of the plan. Destroy the pages replaced and insert the new pages. Note the change in the Amendment Sheet (A1.1). Update copies of the plan which are stored off site, and nominate a person responsible for ensuring this is done.

Distribution

The plan is in sections. This allows copying of relevant sections of the plan to officers, who do not need the complete plan. Treat the plan as a security document and as such control its distribution and access.

Copies have been distributed as follows:

Function	Sections

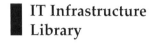
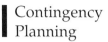
When a Disaster Happens

The decision whether and, if so, how to invoke the disaster recovery action will be taken by the CP Manager, after assessing the situation and where necessary consulting senior management.

The actions to be taken by members of the disaster recovery team(s) to effect a recovery are contained in this plan. The programme of actions will depend on the length of time the disaster is expected to last, and the amount of damage to the installation. The CP Manager will notify which programme of actions is to be carried out.

How Serious is the Disaster?

It is likely that separate programmes of action (see A1.4) will be devised to cater for different categories of disaster. Typically the severity of the disaster depends on the expected period of outage and the level of damage.

For example

Category	Outage	Damage
Minor	Up to 24 hours	Small
Medium	2-7 days	Partial
Major	more than 7 days	Severe

Introduction

This proforma plan is designed to help the CP Manager to design and produce a workable and comprehensive contingency plan. The proforma plan is a model which can be adapted to fit Departments' particular circumstances.

The proforma plan consists of proforma record layouts with notes for completion and advice on what other information should be included in the actual plan. It is not anticipated that every plan will contain all of the items, or categories, of information listed; discard redundant forms.

The contents of a contingency plan must contain all the information that the CP Manager needs to:

* decide the programme of action to be taken

* initiate the action

* control the continued processing of work as prescribed

* return the operation to normal.

Following a disaster the CP Manager needs to take advice from the teams (A1.3), and then decide on the length of time the IT service is expected to be out of action. Document A1.4 in the proforma plan, "When and how to invoke the plan", contains a list of the actions to be taken, depending on the length of time the service is expected to be unavailable.

Most of the detailed information required for the plan should already be available at the installation (eg Asset Register) or from the Initiation Stage (eg minimum computing facilities): see section 3.1 in the CP Module.

The proforma plan should be used in conjunction with the advice given in the CP module to develop a specific IT Contingency Plan.

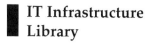
Sections of the Contingency Plan

The Plan is divided into 7 sections.   **Page**

A1. Administration   **A-5**

This contains information on how and when to invoke the plan; the programmes of action to be entered into; the officers involved and where the emergency control centre is located.

A2. IT Infrastructure   **A-17**

The hardware, telecommunications and software which comprises the replacement system and/or the reorder process are included, together with details of any contracts and agreements entered into in support of recovery and reorder.

A3. IT Infrastructure Management & Operating Procedures   **A-21**

The instructions required to enable an IT (including DPU) facility to recommence operations following an emergency.

Service level agreements are included in this section, and these include any relaxation of requirements that apply during a contingency.

A4. Personnel   **A-29**

Contains information on the officers who transfer to the contingency site and of accommodation available to them if they are unable to return to their home because of the time and distance to be travelled.

A5. Security   **A-31**

This section contains the fire and bomb instructions at the home site, and information on remote storage and the items stored there.

A6. Contingency Site   **A-36**

This section is devoted to information about the location of the contingency site; the people to be contacted there; staff facilities; security; and of transport arrangements.

A7. Return to Normal   **A-42**

This section states the dependencies which influence how return to normal can be achieved, and where possible how this is to be done.

A1.1 Administration - Amendment Sheet

CHANGE No	DATE	Initials	CHANGE No	DATE	Initials

Use this form to record authorized amendments made to the document.

Initiate changes by the Department's change control system. Changes will also be initiated by the CP Manager through formal plan reviews (which are also subject to normal change control).

Insert the change number and the date on which the change is made, together with your initials.

A1.2 Administration - Incident/Action Log

DATE	TIME	INCIDENT	ACTION TAKEN	COVERED BY PLAN?

Log any incident which causes, or occurs during, an emergency. Note the action taken; by whom; and whether the event had been anticipated and catered for in the plan.

The log contains

* a sequence of events in chronological order for reference and reporting purposes

* help for another officer to take control of the disaster recovery operation, if required

* information which can assist in any post-disaster reappraisal of the adequacy of the plan and possible revision.

The log must be produced by the Contingency Planning Manager (or his representative).

A1.3 Administration - Disaster Team

TEAM	MEMBERS	RESPONSIBILITY

To make the most productive use of staff in an emergency they should be organized into recovery teams and given specific areas of responsibility, and tasks to perform.

Typical teams, and their component members, should include:

* **Management Team**

   IT Services Manager
   Contingency Planning Manager
   Personnel Manager
   Finance Officer

* **Facilities and Security Team**

   Configuration Manager
   Office Services
   Personnel Services
   Departmental Security Officer
   Welfare

IT Services Teams, under the direction of the IT Services Manager and the Contingency Planning Manager, as follows:

* **Operations Team**

  Operations Manager
  Shift Leader(s)
  Operations/Technical Support

* **Telecommunications Team**

  Network Manager
  Support Staff

* **Data Preparation Team**

  Data Preparation Manager
  Data Preparation Supervisor

* **Recovery & Service Quality Team**

  Database & Software Recovery Manager
  Configuration Manager
  Change/Problem Manager
  User Liaison Manager
  Service Level Manager
  Help Desk
  Technical Support

The above list is not definitive and teams should be constructed to best suit the needs of the organization.

For small organizations, combine a number of the tasks to be handled by a smaller number of teams, or even by one team, as appropriate.

Nominate substitutes for every team member, and inform them of their responsibilities in an emergency situation.

A1.4 Administration - When & How to Invoke the Plan

There is no proforma for this item

The decision to implement the recovery programme is the responsibility of the Director of IT but may be delegated to the Contingency Planning Manager. The degree to which it is implemented depends on the severity of the break/disaster and the estimated time to restore the service. The sequence and timing of actions depends upon the criticality of the systems, be they online or batch. (An analysis of criticality is included in the Initiation Stage).

Produce a timetable of events showing the sequence of actions to be taken, depending on the estimated length of the loss of the system.

Subdivide the timetable to show

a)   the immediate actions to be taken and

b)   the longer term actions required to bring the home site back to normal.

The team responsiblity for the action will also be shown.

Produce timetables for the three catagories of disaster, examples of which are given in the Preface (minor < 24 hours, medium 2-7 days, major > 7 days). Examples of the first two timetables are given below.

EXAMPLE: TIMETABLE 1

The system is expected to be up and running again within 24 hours.

ACTIONS - IMMEDIATE	TEAM RESPONSIBLE
Place contingency contractors on standby	Management
Call in the engineers	IT Services
Establish whether to wait or go to contingency site	Management
Inform T/U Side	Management
Inform users of situation (via Help Desk)	IT Services
If at any time during the 24 hour period the estimated length of the outage exceeds 24 hours go to the next Timetable.	Management
When computer is operational again process outstanding work.	IT Services
Take Contingency contractors off standby	Management.

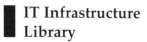
EXAMPLE TIMETABLE 2

The service is expected to be up and running again within 7 days.

ACTIONS - IMMEDIATE

Call in the engineers	IT Services
Contact contingency contractors	Management
Proceed to contingency site	Facilities
Inform T/U Side	Management
Inform users (via Help Desk)	IT Services
Invoke Contingency Plan	Management

ACTIONS - LONGER TERM

Plan return to home site	Management
Ensure SLA's maintained	IT Services
Maintain record of actions	Management
Record any processing backlog	IT Services
Release contingency contractors	Management
Pay contingency contractors	Management
Process backlog	IT Services
Report to higher management	Management
Review contingency plan	Management

The above are examples of timetables of actions to be carried out at particular times.

Departments: produce your own timetables based on:

* the criticality of the estimated length of outage
* the team responsibilities
* the actions deemed necessary.

The following are checklists of actions and responsibilities following an emergency.

MANAGEMENT TEAM

Move to the emergency control centre

Request an assessment of the problem (eg 999 services or security staff)

Contact the contingency contractors to place them on standby

Report to senior management (verbal)

Inform the recovery team leaders, and call a meeting to:

*   ascertain the nature of the problem, the extent of the disruption, the consequences and likely implications

*   agree team plans to be put into action immediately.

Act as main points of contact with emergency services and the media (via press officer)

Where the course of action is not obvious, allow an agreed period of time in which further information can be gathered on the severity of the problem and the likely period of outage.

Call another meeting to

*   receive reports from team leaders

*   decide whether to invoke the plan

*   agree plans for each team to be reviewed at an agreed time.

Contact the contingency contractors either to arrange to use their services (eg a transfer to their facility), to update them on the situation or to release them.

Initiate plans for transfer to the contingency site

Report progress and plans to senior management

Following the move - at the contingency site:

*   manage relations with contractors

*   ensure the service levels contracted for with the users are provided

*   ensure IT management procedures are adhered to

*   monitor, and where necessary set in motion, plans for returning the processing to a permanent home site

*   ensure any personnel problems are dealt with.

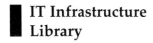
Following return:

> *   review the plan
>
> *   produce a final report to management
>
> *   oversee the work of the other teams; ensure they report back regularly; tackle any problems that they are unable to resolve for themselves.

FACILITIES AND SECURITY TEAM

Attend the initial meeting called by the Management Team

Attend to any staff problems resulting from the disaster

Conduct an asset inventory to include an evaluation of damaged equipment and equipment to be replaced, and update the configuration management database as necessary.

Make the site secure and carry out safety checks. Assess damage and time needed to replace accommodation and environmental services.

If the decision is taken to move to the contingency site:

> *   arrange hotel or other temporary accommodation
>
> *   arrange hiring etc of transport
>
> *   help with transfer of staff.

Following the move - at the contingency site:

> *   ensure all administrative support services such as typing, fax, telex, messengers, mail, office equipment are provided
>
> *   set up security procedures and access for staff (physical & logical)
>
> *   contact suppliers of essential services to connect supplies eg electricity, water, telephones
>
> *   provide any office supplies
>
> *   arrange for the transfer of media and other items from back up store to the contingency site and the setting up of another temporary back up site if required
>
> *   attend to any staff problems as a result of the move.

This team must prepare as soon as practicable, for the transfer back to the home site.

IT SERVICES TEAMS

Consult with computer engineers.

Attend the initial meeting called by the management team.

Contact all operations, operations/technical support, data preparation, data control, job control and output handling staff:

*   to appraise them of the problem and the initial actions being taken

*   to make sure they know what to do.

Inform users, via the help desk, of the problems and the plans for informing them of a resumption of service.

If a decision is taken to move to the contingency site:

*   contact suppliers of replacement machinery and ancillary equipment. Inform them of the move and order equipment

*   brief all staff who are to transfer to the contingency site

*   arrange with the Facilities and Security Team the transfer of staff and essential documentation to the contingency site, and the backup media and other items from the backup store.

Inform users of the current situation.

Following the move - at the contingency site.

In conjunction with the Facilities and Security Team, monitor the delivery and installation of any equipment.

Accept handover of the facility after initialising and testing the hardware, operating system and telecommunications networks (in conjunction with other teams).

Prepare production schedules

Take security copies of all files before commencing processing.

Transfer security copies to new temporary back up site.

Recover the service and start processing of work in accordance with the schedule. Ensure technical support are on hand to iron out any problems.

Ensure infrastructure management disciplines are maintained (eg performance and serviceability monitoring, capacity, change, problem and security management). Ensure service level agreements are honoured.

This team will need to shedule the processing of any backlog of accumulated work following transfer to the contingency site (and on return to home site).

The preceding paragraphs contain detailed check lists for the teams that are likely to have heavy involvement in the work associated with a disaster, and the recovery from it. Departments: adapt these to fit your own situations.

Identify additionally other functions (eg admin) as necessary, set up teams and produce check lists of actions and responsibilities they have to carry out.

A1.5 Administration - Emergency Contacts(Internal)

NAME	ORGANIZATION/ RESPONSIBILITY	TELEPHONE No		HOME ADDRESS
		Office	Home	

List the name, section and telephone number of officers within the building or organisation for ease of communication:

- * security
- * engineers
- * electricians
- * heating/aircon engineers
- * Office Services
- * first aid
- * welfare

A1.6 Administration - Officers Who Have a Copy of the Plan

NAME	LOCATION	PHONE No	RESPONSIBILITY	SECTIONS HELD All/Part Only

Generate a list of officers who have a copy of the plan. If a copy of the plan is destroyed or is rendered inaccessible by an emergency this list will make it easier to acquire a replacement copy. Keep a number of up-to-date copies stored in a secure location off-site in case the disaster results in access to the building, or parts of it, being denied.

Use the list to serve as a distribution list for amendments.

A1.7 Administration - Location of Emergency Control Centre(s)

LOCATION	ADDRESS	TEL No

In the event of a disaster, set up an Emergency Control Centre (ECC) for the Contingency Planning Manager and the Management Team to meet there as soon as the disaster occurs. Direct all activity and communication from the ECC throughout the disaster and undertake from there the work needed to return to normal.

This centre is about controlling the disaster, not managing the contingency site.

Ensure the ECC is easily accessible, secure, and as close as possible to the affected facility. Give consideration to locating an ECC close to the home site but, where possible, in a separate building. Where the ECC is located at the home site, Departments should make provision for an alternative control centre in case the main one is not available.

Ensure the ECC is fully equiped, with normal office facilities including telephone(s). Store copies of the plan securely in the room at all times.

File a map of the location of the ECC here.

A2.1 IT Infrastructure - Service Contractors

NAME	ORGANIZATION & Service Provided	TEL No	CONTACT

List service contractors and maintenance companies which may be contacted to supply services or equipment associated with recovery

* computer equipment suppliers

* telecomms equipment suppliers

* data entry equipment suppliers

* software suppliers

* output processing

* machinery removal

* equipment cleaning

* accommodation cleaning

* off site media and/or plan storage

* hot site provider

* cold site provider

* processing/data entry bureau.

A2.2 IT Infrastructure - Asset Register

There is no proforma for this item.

Ensure the installation's asset register is available from the configuration management section. Further information on asset registers is available in the IT Infrastructure Library module on Configuration Management. Use this register to help the reorder process for hardware damaged or destroyed together with any necessary software.

Include:

> * computer hardware
> * telecommunications equipment
> * data processing equipment
> * output processing equipment
> * software, including version numbers.

If a minimum configuration would be an acceptable way to proceed for an interim period, direct attention to the next section.

A2.3 IT Infrastructure - Minimum Computing Facilities

There is no proforma for this item.

These are the facilities required, hardware, software and telecommunications to provide an interim service, based on processing only the critical applications on a smaller system. This information is/has been used to identify suitable contingency services available and/or to order replacement facilities.

Use the same layout as the asset register for this purpose.

See A3.1 for configuration details.

A2.4 IT Infrastructure - Contracts & Agreements

There is no proforma for this item.

File copies of all contracts and agreements relating to existing or replacement items here.

Include:

*   hot start suppliers (fixed & portable)
*   cold start suppliers (fixed & portable)
*   bureau(x)
*   dormant contracts (if used)
*   software licence agreements.

A3.1 IT Infrastructure Management & Operating Procedures - IT Infrastructure Management

There is no proforma for this item.

Ensure all IT Infrastructure Management procedures and support documentation are available at the contingency site (eg service level, change, problem, configuration management. See specific IT Infrastructure Library modules for more details).

A3.2 IT Infrastructure Management & Operating Procedures - Service Level Agreements

There is no proforma for this item.

Copy and file all Service Level Agreements here. It is possible that special conditions apply in a contingency situation; include details of these in the SLA.

A3.3 IT Infrastructure Management & Operating Procedures - Operations Manual

There is no proforma for this item.

Ensure the Operations Manual reflects the conditions as they obtain at the contingency site, and include instructions on:

*   powering up and down

*   system loading and unloading

*   peripheral configuration

*   peripheral handling and cleaning

*   media handling

*   system breaks/incidents and what to do

*   scheduled/unscheduled maintenance

*   environmental monitoring eg. what to do when the power trips out or the air conditioning fails

*   network map & necessary strappings

*   anything else which will be different for Operations at the contingency site.

Ensure the manual contains copies of all computer, data preparation and network configurations. (NB Give special consideration to configuration details when minimum computing facilities are being used.)

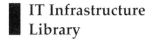

A3.4 IT Infrastructure Management & Operating Procedures - Processing Schedules

There is no proforma for this item.

Note: these schedules already exist if the complete workload is being transferred to the contingency site, but produce a selected subset if only the critical work is to be processed.

Carry out any recovery work required when work is transferred to a contingency site, particularly if media have been damaged or destroyed. The amount of recovery depends on how often the files are backed up and the amount of work done since the backup. Include instructions on how to carry out this recovery task in this section. When that recovery task is complete, schedule the work to run in its proper sequence.

These schedules will have been produced to the Department's own standards and layout.

A3.5 IT Infrastructure Management & Operating Procedures - Service/Job Operating Instructions

There is no proforma for this item.

Ensure a copy of the Job Operating instructions exists for each service/job which is to be run at the contingency site (see the Contingency Planning module section 4.1 for further details).

Include information on:

* input
* parameters
* console messages, and how to respond to them
* restarting
* magnetic media
* expected output
* output handling
* support any procedures & contacts.

Include copies of end-user procedures/notices that are different in a contingency situation.

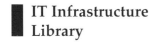
A3.6 IT Infrastructure Management & Operating Procedures - Data Entry Procedures

There is no proforma for this item.

Reproduce any specific procedures for inputting data into the system, including direct data entry via terminals or PCK only if they are not included as part of separate job instructions.

Produce separate data entry procedures if a Data Prep Bureau is to be used in a contingency situation (see A2.1 and A2.4).

A3.7 IT Infrastructure Management & Operating Procedures - Output Processing

JOB	FORM NO/ OUTPUT IDENTITY	QUANTITY	PAPER/OTHER PROCESS

If special handling processes are required, detail them here.

Note: this is particularly important if processing of output:

*   is to be transferred to a bureau

*   is to be handled at a site away from the computer processing

*   where the job operating instructions cannot be released eg for security reasons.

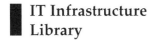

A3.8 IT Infrastructure Management & Operating Procedures - Clerical Procedures

There is no proforma for this item.

Input copies of any clerical procedures which are to be used as an alternative to, or to complement, computer systems here, similarly if jobs already exist which require an element of clerical work eg. job preparation and submission.

A4.1 Personnel - Officers Transferred to Contingency Site

NAME	GRADE	JOB	LOCATION AT CONTINGENCY SITE	
			ROOM	Tel No

List those officers to be transferred temporarily to the contingency site to provide a useful record:

*   for Personnel and pay purposes

*   for arranging transport

*   for ease of contact

*   to assess if sufficient personnel are available following the disaster

*   for security purposes.

Wherever possible, attempt to identify the exact individuals (eg where shift workers are involved) and ensure the tasks to be carried out and the staff numbers involved are detailed.

A4.2 Personnel - Accommodation/Hotels etc

TYPE OF ACCOMMODATION	ADDRESS	Tel No	CHARGES

Where residential accommodation is required provide a list of suitable establishments, with maps showing where they are located. Usual sources for this information are tourist information offices and/or people working at the contingency site.

Assign the Facilities and Security Team responsibility for booking accommodation in an emergency situation, after first checking the type, and cost, required.

A5.1 Security - Fire & Bomb Instructions

There is no proforma for this item.

Insert a copy of the fire and bomb instructions telling staff what to do, and where to go, when the alarms are sounded.

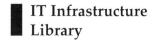
A5.2 Security - First Aid

There is no proforma for this item.

Provide instructions on the first aid/medical facilities available including:

* *   names and locations of trained officers
* *   location of "rest" room
* *   location of medical supplies
* *   first aid during shift working.

Insert the instructions here.

A5.3 Security - Emergency Service Contacts

NAME	ORGANIZATION/RESPONSIBILITY	TEL No

Insert here the names of public utilities and departments which may be contacted to provide emergency action with the names of individuals if known, and where to contact them:

* Fire Service

* Police

* Medical Services (including hospitals)

* Electricity

* Gas

* Water

* Drainage

* BT/Mercury

* PSA

* Insurance

* Air Conditioning Maintainer.

A5.4 Security - Location of/Access to Remote Stores

COMPANY/ROOM/SAFE	ADDRESS	CONTACT	TEL No

Record the location of any company, or other departmental facility, used for the security storage of items, together with a map of the location.

A5.5 Security - Items Stored at Remote Site

ITEM	DESCRIPTION	QUANTITY	MEDIA IDENTITY

Record the items stored remotely as follows:

Backup Media

A record of the tapes and discs copied regularly, with discmaps and filenames etc to facilitate identification and transporting to the contingency site.

Stationery

The types of stationery and quantities stored.

Computer cleaning materials

It may be necessary to store such materials, particularly if they are not available at the contingency site, or they cannot be obtained quickly.

Blank media

If blank media is needed eg. for carrying out security copying at the contingency site.

Replacement equipment

If spare items of kit are stored remotely.

Documentation

Copies of the contingency plan, source code listings etc.

A6.1 Contingency Site - Location

NAME ADDRESS   Tel No(s) FAX No
BUS ROUTE(S) STATION LOCAL TAXI Tel No(s)

Write all information on where the site is and how to get there here, together with a map showing the exact location and points of entry and any special requirements to gain access eg security pass, telephone authority.

A6.2 Contingency Site - Contacts

NAME	TITLE/SECTION	Tel No	ROOM No

List all permanent officers at the contingency site, who may need to be contacted:

*   to arrange testing
*   for information relating to their procedures
*   immediately after a disaster.

A6.3 Contingency Site - Staff Facilities

FACILITY	DETAIL

Provide those facilities which are essential for staff in any workplace eg. washing and toilet facilities, heating and lighting and also certain minimum space requirements.

Provide the following facilities for the convenience of staff at your contingency location:

*   parking

*   restaurant/canteen facilities

*   recreation facilities.

If staff are expected to work and stay at a location some distance away from their normal office, then include information on services and facilities available at or near that location here.

A6.4 Contingency Site - Security

There is no proforma for this item.

Ensure these instructions are available:

*   *   entry to the building
*   *   entry to controlled areas
*   *   access to systems
*   *   emergency procedures including fire and bomb warnings and evacuation procedures
*   *   first aid facilities.

A6.5 Contingency Site - Transport

TYPE OF VEHICLE /PURPOSE	COMPANY	Tel No

Provide transport as required for carrying:

*   staff
*   media
*   supplies
*   mail
*   input/output.

Record the type of transport required and the companies which can provide the services.

A6.6 Contingency Site - People/Items to be Transported

PEOPLE/ITEMS	QUANTITY/ NUMBER	WHEN	FROM	TO

Record the people and other items which will need transporting, how often eg. daily, weekly, once only and the pickup and putdown locations.

A7 Return to Normal

EXTENT OF DAMAGE	PREDICTED DURATION OF OUTAGE
PROPOSED CORRECTIVE ACTION	RESPONSIBILITY

Note that the guidance given in the module states that returning to normal largely depends on a number of things which can not be predicted. However enter here what actions can be planned with certainty in advance, for each of the timetables previously mentioned (eg minor <24 hours, medium 2-7 days, major > 7 days).

Actions depend on:

*   extent and nature of disaster (how much damage)

*   duration of outage

*   processing of backlog.

After returning to the home site, the Contingency Planning Manager will conduct a review of the contingency operation, assess the effectiveness of the plan, instigate any changes to it, and report to senior management.

Example

EXTENT OF DAMAGE	PREDICTED DURATION OF OUTAGE
Total destruction of IT installation by fire.	18 months

PROPOSED CORRECTIVE ACTION	RESPONSIBILITY
Immediate	
Clear site	PSA
Salvage machinery	Office Services
Dispose of scrap machinery	Office Services
Reappraise equipment needs	IT Strategy group
Reappraise accommodation needs, human/equipment	IT Strategy group
Redesign building	PSA
Tenders for new buildings	PSA
Supervise new building work	PSA
Some time later	
Acquire equipment	Contracts
(Re)train staff	Training / hardware supplier
Site trials and handover	IT Services Manager
Transfer services from contingency site	IT Services teams

Annex B. CRAMM Overview

Introduction

This Annex describes CRAMM, the CCTA Risk Analysis and Management Methodology for the identification of justified security measures for both current and future Information Technology (IT) systems processing Government sensitive data.

CRAMM was developed, with assistance from BIS Applied Systems Ltd, by the CCTA IT Security and Privacy Group - the National Authority for advising Government Departments on all aspects of the protection of IT systems handling unclassified but sensitive data.

Background to Risk Analysis and Management

The security of IT systems and data processed, stored or transported by them has been of major concern to Government Departments for many years, and some systems demonstrate a more stringent approach to IT security than can be found elsewhere in the UK.

Indeed, to determine these levels of security, Departments have recognized and used the general concepts of risk analysis and management for some time and implemented them in a pragmatic and potentially subjective manner.

However, by mid 1985 both Departments and the Government Security Authorities identified the need to develop a unified approach to risk analysis and management which was threat rather than vulnerability driven and which could be applied across the wide range of Government system types to identify more accurately necessary security countermeasures, provide justification for spend and be understandable to non-expert general managers.

With the rapid expansion of IT and the high cost of development of some secure systems it was not considered viable to continue with a significant probability of unjustified spend on security and/or without high confidence that all justified countermeasures were identified.

Thus, it was agreed that risk analysis and management should be put on a much more formal and structured basis to deal with these problems using as a basepoint the main components of risk analysis and management as described below.

General Concepts of Risk Analysis and Management

Much has been written on the topic of risk analysis and management, and it is therefore necessary to define some of the general assumptions behind the specific approach for government IT systems. The term 'risk analysis and management' emphasises the need for a comprehensive approach and encompasses two major activities - risk analysis and risk management.

Risk analysis involves the identification and valuation of assets (both physical - for example computer hardware units, and data - for example sensitive computer-held information on Government contracts), the identification and determination of the levels of threats (both accidental and deliberate) to the identified assets, and the identification and determination of the levels of vulnerabilities of the identified assets that might be exploited by the identified threats.

These three factors - asset values, threat and vulnerability levels - are used to calculate the levels of risks to the assets. This process recognizes that there has to be some motivation for certain types of threat (ie deliberate 'attack') to be translated into actions which could have an impact on the assets and that such impact may range from insignificant to catastrophic.

Risk management involves reducing the vulnerability of assets through the adoption of countermeasures. Such countermeasures may act in different ways. They may reduce the risk of a threat occurring, reduce the impact of an occurrence, detect an occurrence, or enable recovery from an occurrence.

Overall, IT Security Risk Analysis and Management can be expressed by the simple model:-

Figure B-1:
General Concepts

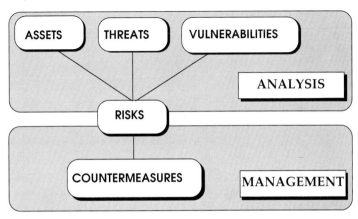

Thus the components of Risk Analysis and Management are:-

a) **ASSET IDENTIFICATION AND VALUATION** - the
identification and valuation of an IT system's physical and
data assets, to determine the effects if vulnerabilities were
exploited by threats, in terms of the impacts of disclosure,
modification, unavailability and destruction.

b) **THREAT ASSESSMENT** - the identification, and
assessment of the likelihood of unwanted, deliberate or
accidental, incidents impacting on IT systems.

c) **VULNERABILITY ASSESSMENT** - the assessment of the
extent to which IT systems could be susceptible to identified
threats.

d) **RISK ASSESSMENT** - the assessment of the levels of risks
indicated by the determined levels of threats and potential
vulnerabilities, and values of assets.

e) **COUNTERMEASURE SELECTION** - the selection of
security countermeasures justified by, and to reduce to an
acceptable level, the levels of risks assessed at (d).

Thus (a) to (d) are termed **RISK ANALYSIS**, and (e) **RISK
MANAGEMENT**.

HMG Approach

As a National IT Security Authority for Government Departments, CCTA was invited to mount and manage a project to identify or develop a risk analysis and management methodology which would meet thirteen mandatory requirements. These included:-

* "able to deal with Government Operational and Administrative systems of all sizes";

* "able to encompass all technical (for example, Hardware, Software, Communications) and non-technical (for example, Physical, Personnel) aspects of IT security";

* "compatible with existing Government IT Security guidance";

* "suitable for use during the development of a system, ie for projects as well as existing installations";

* "easy to use, after training, by staff with IT but not necessarily IT security experience";

* "able to be used such that reviews can be carried out quickly enough to ensure that results are not overtaken by changes in the system;

* "able to be used with an automated support tool";

* "able to present results for management in a readily understandable form".

The first task was to examine existing methodologies to determine if any existed which could be taken directly for Government use.

Several methodologies were identified; however none met all the mandatory requirements. Whilst at first glance Annual Loss Expectancy (ALE) based quantitative approaches seemed attractive, it became evident that the inevitably subjective way in which figures are attributed, particularly costs for data assets, could produce an unsound baseline and inconsistencies between similar reviews.

Also these methodologies typically did not offer much support for countermeasure selection with a consequential need for the reviewer to have IT security knowledge, coupled with the fact that analysis could be lengthy.

Existing qualitative methodologies were either insufficiently rigorous, did not cover all main components of risk management or were not sufficiently far enough advanced to be of use.

Therefore it was decided that Government requirements could only be met by devising a new methodology following a qualitative approach, but wherever possible taking quantitative input, and containing no 'hidden' logic.

Accordingly, CRAMM with its automated support tool was developed and successfully trailed with both Administrative and Operational, and existing and planned, systems.

The automated support tool was developed not only to assist the reviewer in the clerical effort of carrying out a review but also to:

- considerably shorten review times through reviewer help screens and automatic calculation (for example, of required countermeasures)

- produce better and consistent management reports

- provide facilities to answer 'what if' questions, which wouldbe time-consuming or impossible with a manual or purely paper based methodology.

After the successful trials the CRAMM 'product' was assembled:-

- documentation, including management and user guide;

- an automated support tool, for use on IBM or compatible PCs;

- a training course run at the Civil Service College.

The 'product' launch and first course were in January 1988. CRAMM is now the 'Preferred' methodology for the identification of justified security countermeasures for the protection of IT systems processing Government unclassified but sensitive data.

Overview of the Methodology

The methodology comprises a staged, or modular, approach. The first two stages address analysis of the risk and the third and final one addresses management of risks through the implementation of countermeasures.

Each stage is supported by questionnaires and guidelines and sets out to answer one major question. Simply stated these are:-

Stage 1: is there a security need above a certain baseline level?

Stage 2: where and what is the extent of the security need?

Stage 3: how can this need be met?

Stage 1

The first part of Stage 1 is the important task of precisely determining the nature and boundaries of the system under review, and identifying its various components.

This is accomplished by the acquisition of information on the user community and the manner in which they use, or will use, the system - together with an outline system configuration diagram.

This information is obtained from interviews with senior installation or project and user managers, and their staff, and is essential in providing the reviewer with the understanding necessary for the specific boundary of the review to be agreed and later for the questionnaires and guidelines to be put into perspective. It also provides sufficient detail, for instance on the number of 'owners' of (and/or those who can speak authoritatively about) data for the review to be scheduled.

Stage 1 then continues with its major function - the determination of qualitative values for assets, both physical and data. The CRAMM documentation provides detailed advice on how the reviewer should schedule for, conduct and record interviews with data 'owners' and personnel responsible for physical assets, and to review results with system or project management.

A carefully structured questionnaire enables the reviewer to establish the selection of qualitative data asset values, without 'user bias', for the four possible impacts of disclosure, modification, unavailability in terms of three time periods and destruction, by both accidental and deliberate means.

This selection is aided by detailed 'common metric' guidance for data valuation covering such issues as political embarrassment, commercial confidentiality, personal privacy, personal safety, financial and legal implications.

For example, if the data contains details of legal contracts, a reviewer will ask what the effect would be of the organization being in breach of contract. Would it be sued? For how much? What would the effect of the publicity be? The guidelines will relate this to a scale of 1 to 10.

All the physical assets that comprise the system under review such as hardware, air conditioning plant and documentation are identified to produce as asset register and then valued in terms of replacement or reconstruction costs. These values are then converted onto the same qualitative scale as that used for data assets.

An advantage of the methodology is that time and resource wastage can be avoided where all values are low.

In these circumstances what is in effect an abbreviated version of Stage 2 would be used to check whether there are any threats, vulnerabilities, or combinations thereof, which are of sufficient level to justify greater than baseline protection for low value assets. If the value of all assets is low then only baseline protection (or a "code of good practice") is justified, and a review will move directly to Stage 3. Only where asset values are medium or high is Stage 2 recommended.

At the end of Stage 1, as with the subsequent two stages, there is a comprehensive management review.

Stage 2

The extent of the security needed by a system relates not just to values of assets but also to the levels and nature of threats to which the system could be subjected and the likely vulnerabilites of the system assets to those threats.

The first part of Stage 2 is concerned with evaluating the dependency of a system or potential system on certain assets. The reviewer then records which physical assets are required in order for each application or data group to successfully function.

Physical assets are then organised, for the purpose of threat and vulnerability assessment, into groups. This is carried out in order to save time in that a number of physical assets in the same area may be vulnerable to the same threats eg fire.

More than twenty generic threat types, for example fire, water damage, system infiltration and misuse of resources, are then used as the basis to assess the qualitative threat and vulnerability levels per relevant asset group, using pairs of structured questionnaires incorporating the knowledge of Government Security experts.

As far as possible questions are framed so as to prompt a "yes" or "no" answer to avoid bias, with each answer afforded a particular score; total scores per questionnaire indicate a high, medium, or low threat or vulnerability.

For each relevant asset group, the combination of asset value and assessments of the levels of vulnerabilities and threats are used to calculate a security requirement (ie risk) number on a scale of one (baseline) to five, for each of the four possible impacts (ie disclosure, modification, unavailability and destruction).

At the end of Stage 2, management has a clear view of the levels of threats to, vulnerabilities of, and thus risks to, particular asset groups. The expression of risks in a numerical form enables direct matching to countermeasures in Stage 3.

The completed analysis of risks, ie at the end of Stage 2, is reviewed in detail with management before moving to Stage 3.

Stage 3

Stage 3 determines how the identified security need can be met, ie countermeasure selection. This is an area which appears to have received relatively little attention in other methodologies, yet the task of selecting countermeasures is a formidable one.

For example, a major installation or network may require several hundred countermeasures to be implemented. These could range from a hot start contingency site to procedures to assign passwords, to check controls over input data, to encryption, to fire extinguishers in the general office. The range is enormous, making selection extremely difficult.

Taking the determined levels of risks, ie the security requirement numbers, for each asset grouping, countermeasures (covering all aspects of security) are selected from a large 'library' which is grouped by among other things security aspect (for example Physical, Personnel, Software, Communications) and is further annotated by type, eg. reduce risk, reduce impact, detect. If the review is of a current installation, details of existing countermeasures are now recorded. (This activity is deliberately kept until the end of the review to avoid prejudging the effectiveness and/or justified need for existing countermeasures.)

A comparison is conducted to ascertain which additional countermeasures are to be recommended, and which existing ones are not justified. As the list of countermeasures is produced, it is annotated with likely levels of cost (from information held in the 'library'). Then costs specific to the actual or likely equipment types can be added, and a further management review is held.

If management is unhappy about some aspect, for example, the likely overall cost is outside the budget, 'what if' questions can be dealt with (for example, what would be the effect of removing one very time critical data group to a different stand alone machine). In other words a parameter can be changed and the methodology re-run to determine the effect.

The final step is to determine when a further review should be carried out. (For example periodic and/or after a significant configuration change). Much of the information gathered during a first review can be used in, and thus greatly speed up, subsequent reviews.

Conclusion

Thus to conclude, the main CRAMM concepts are:-

- baseline level of countermeasures;

- common metric guidance for qualitative valuation of data assets for the four major impacts;

- the identification and qualitative valuation of physical assets;

- no presumptions made as to the need for previously implemented countermeasures;

- the identification of the dependencies on physical assets;

- qualitative assessment of threat types against specific groups of assets;

- qualitative assessment of the vulnerabilities of these specific groups of assets;

- combination of qualitative values for assets and threat and vulnerability ratings to form numeric indications of risks;

- matching numeric indications of risks to specific countermeasures;

- for an existing installation identifying not only justified but also unjustified countermeasures.

It is now clear that formal risk analysis and management is a prerequisite for the development of a contingency plan.

The information collected during a CRAMM review could be used to establish the type of contingency plan required, identify particular evaluation needs and to construct the contingency and as well as security policy and requirement documents.

Indeed, the methodology will be invaluable to management in presenting easily understandable results in the form of countermeasure lists justified in accordance with the real security need (and for existing installations identifying countermeasures which may not be justified and could be removed - probably with cost savings and easing of operational constraint).

Management will thus be able to consider submissions for money spend on security supported by a logical, properly-constructed and justified case.

For further information on CRAMM please contact:

CCTA Library
Rosebery Court
St Andrews Business Park
NORWICH
NR7 0HS

Telephone 01603 704 930
GTN 3040 4930

It should be noted that the CCTA methodology, CRAMM, is
crown Copyright, and "CRAMM" is Trademark applied for.

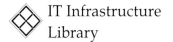

IT Infrastructure
Library

Comments Sheet
Contingency Planning ▌

CCTA hopes that you find this book both useful and interesting. We will welcome your comments and suggestions for improving it.
Please use this form or a photocopy, and continue on a further sheet if needed.

From:

        Name

        Organization

        Address

        Telephone

re: **Issue 1**
     March 1989

COVERAGE
Does the material cover your needs?
If not, then what additional material would you like included.

CLARITY
Are there any points which are unclear?
If yes, please detail where and why.

ACCURACY
Please give details of any inaccuracies found.

If more space is required for these or other comments, please continue overleaf.

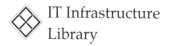

RECEIPT

Do you know of any other person within your
organization who would like a copy of this book?

OTHER COMMENTS

Return to: **CCTA Library**
Rosebery Court
St Andrews Business Park
NORWICH, NR7 0HS

Annex C. Example Terms of Reference - Preliminary Stage

The Task
Report to Senior Management the risks to which the IT service is exposed; actions that can reduce the risks; and contingency planning options to safeguard the continued provision of the IT service. The report will recommend a preferred option and provide relative costings.

Timescale
The report to be produced within 3 calendar months of the Project Team being set up.

Resources
People

  1 x SEO (or consultant) Project Manager - full time
  1 x HEO - full time

Equipment etc required

  1 x IBM PC
  1 copy of CRAMM package

Finance

  £15,000 to include:
    travel and subsistence
    purchase of CRAMM package
    training and consultancy

Task stages
CRAMM training

Identify and value physical and data assets

Evaluation of threats, vulnerabilities and risks

Selection of countermeasures

Investigation of commercial CP services available, and costs

Final version of report

Management reviews
The Project Manager will report progress to the Management Board after each stage, or after 2 weeks, whichever is the sooner.

Annex D. Investment Appraisal for Contingency Planning Measures

We suggest that you undertake a CRAMM study of your IT systems before looking in detail at different contingency planning options. Annex B provides an overview of the CRAMM methodology.

CRAMM does not try to place explicit monetary values on data assets nor on the costs of disruption associated with a loss of service, nor does it try to assign probabilities to the risks to the system. This is because experience of methodologies using a quantitative/money-based approach has indicated that such an approach is fraught with difficulties and can be misleading. Instead CRAMM identifies and values assets, and assesses the threats, vulnerabilities and so risks associated with each component of an IT system all in a qualitative way.

The result of this process enables CRAMM to suggest a series of countermeasures which are appropriate to the degree of risks and 'value' of assets involved.

CRAMM therefore does not provide an identifiable monetary benefit from applying each suggested countermeasure to manage the level of risk. However, it is based on the experience of Government security experts and the results of a significant trials programme encompassing many types of system; thus the implied broad level of expenditure arising from the countermeasures proposed for any system, should be taken as broadly justified on the basis of past experience.

It should be noted that CRAMM does enable the attribution of costs to the justified countermeasures once they have been identified.

Whilst for most aspects of security CRAMM provides a list of detailed countermeasures, for obvious reasons it cannot indicate those provided by specific vendors.

Also, currently CRAMM does not go to a great level of detail for specific contingency planning countermeasures (but it is planned to enhance CRAMM in this respect by April 1989.) Hence, after a CRAMM review is carried out a series of carefully costed options will need to be worked up (that broadly accord with the level of contingency planning suggested by CRAMM), using the CRAMM 'what if' question exploration facility if necessary. In effect, this amounts to conducting a cost effectiveness analysis of options to provide a given level of security to an IT system.

The overall need for a given level of contingency measures can be demonstrated to management by using CRAMM's 'backtrack' facility. This enables the user to determine which were the key factors (eg value of assets, level of risk) that led to the suggested level of countermeasures proposed.

It is inevitable that each set of countermeasures examined is likely to provide a slightly different level of security. Ultimately, in many cases, management will therefore have to take an informed decision, based on the management help facilities provided with CRAMM including that which will enable priorities to be put on justified countermeasures. It should be noted that it would be a management decision not to implement a particular sort of countermeasure justified by CRAMM and to take the risk - the possible impact of not implementing a particular countermeasure can be judged by using the 'backtrack' facility.

Further details on investment appraisal for contingency planning are available from the CCTA contact shown in section 9.

The price of this publication has been set to make some contribution to the preparation costs incurred at CCTA.

Printed in the United Kingdom for The Stationery Office
TJ730 3/00 C7 10170